SAILING ON A MICRO-BUDGET

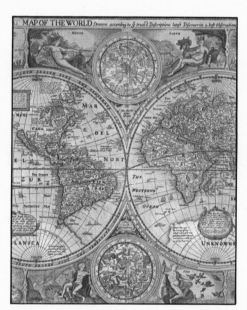

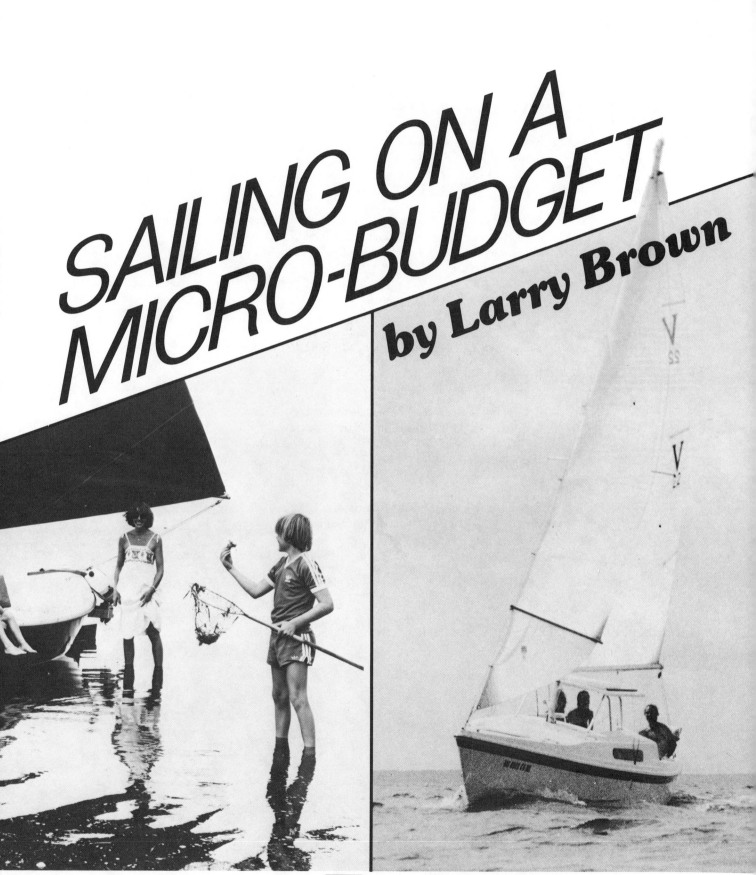

SAILING ON A MICRO-BUDGET

by Larry Brown

Seven Seas Press, Inc. Newport, Rhode Island

SEVEN SEAS PRESS, INC.
524 Thames Street
Newport, Rhode Island 02840
Edited by James R. Gilbert

1 3 5 7 9 TS / TS 0 8 6 4 2

LIBRARY OF CONGRESS CATALOGING IN PUBLICATION DATA

Brown, Larry, 1946–
    Sailing on a Micro-Budget.

    1. Sailing—Finance.   2. Boats and boating—Finance.
I. Title.   II. Title: Sailing on a Micro-Budget.
GV811.B72   1985   797.1′24   84-13951
ISBN 0-915160-80-3

Designed by Irving Perkins Associates
Printed in the United States of America by Thomson-Shore, Inc.

To my parents, from whom I learned the love of sailing . . . to my children Julie and Amber . . . and to Bettina for being the fellow voyager I had always dreamed of.

CONTENTS

Contents

Contents

Contents

THE INVITATION

PART I

THE POSSIBILITIES

The last time we sailed into the harbor at West Falmouth, Massachusetts, our camera was on the fritz and so we missed taking an odd and informative picture. Let me paint it for you.

In the center of the frame, you see our little sailboat, *Fearless*, floating in a sea of crystal blue. In the background, slightly out of focus, is the stone breakwater that shelters West Falmouth from Buzzard's Bay. Two children appear to be walking across the surface of the water towards the boat, one carrying a horseshoe crab the size of a dinner plate, the other gesticulating wildly with her arms. Those are our daughters, Julie and Amber.

"How have we trained our children to walk on water?" you ask. We haven't. They're standing on the bottom. That sailboat, our floating

This is all you need.

home for the weekend, draws only seven inches! You'll notice ours is the only boat in the picture. That's because there isn't another cruising boat in West Falmouth that would dare come in here—or that wouldn't run aground long before it got here. It's a delightful spot and we have it all to ourselves.

Now let me turn my back on my family and on our little sailboat and take another picture, this one of West Falmouth Harbor. I'll need a telephoto lens because we are, as I've explained, rather far from it. West Falmouth, with some fine old homes ranging along the shoreline, is a lovely corner of Buzzard's Bay. In its sheltered harbor you'll see, from our vantage point, a small forest of masts. These masts are connected to a small fleet of some beautiful and expensive cruising boats that rest peacefully at their moorings. You'd think that these boats would be a

The Invitation

hubbub of joyful activity: kids swimming and splashing and sails rattling up the masts . . . but no. There isn't a soul around. All is strangely tranquil. From time to time you'll see some kids slide a Beetle Cat off the sand and go sailing, still it's odd that there's so much here and so little going on. What's even stranger is that, at this moment, similar fleets lie idle across the bay in Marion, in Mattapoisett, at Onset—millions of dollars worth of yachts just sitting at their moorings. Don't be alarmed. Nothing's wrong; nothing has happened. This is normal. Most of these boats are rarely used. Surely they're enjoyed when they *are* used. But the rest of the time they are simply floating symbols—distant Tarzan yells—announcing the financial potency of their owners.

Well, I'll make a confession. I don't have any financial potency. I'm a teacher and my income is modest to an embarrassing extreme. If you can afford to buy this book, you probably make more money than I do. But I've got a boat. We make voyages. We're out sailing and the millionaires are not. What's our secret? I'll tell you. The answer is the subject of this book. Basically it's this: We're out here sailing and swimming because we didn't spend a lot of money on our boat. We couldn't afford to buy a yacht so we didn't. We have a little 15-foot boat with a cabin and a boom tent over the cockpit and we make do. And we have fun.

Let me share with you a fairly well-kept secret. It's so often true we could almost call it a law:

The use a boat gets is in inverse proportion to its size and cost.

If you are not wealthy and you want to go sailing and cruising, you can. My boat cost a little less than four thousand dollars, trailer and everything, brand new. Used boats cost less. Don't assume that the family with the $40,000 yacht is going to have 10 times the fun you will. They won't. You may actually do more sailing, and have more fun, than they—with far fewer worries. Real "riches" are measured not in what you own, but in what you can do.

What *can* you do with a small sailboat? If hardship, discomfort and solitude turn you on, you can cross an ocean in a small boat. It's been done dozens of times now. If you don't mind roughing it a bit you can cruise along thousands of miles of coastlines, exploring hidden waterways out of the reach of larger craft.

With thorough and realistic planning, you can bring your family. Here's a chance for real adventure without the solitude. You can easily haul your lightweight boat overland and put it where you actually want to be, leaving the extended (and often tiresome) passagemaking for boats too heavy to follow suit. Whereas the deeper and heavier yacht has to lie offshore, you can sail right up to a beach and go exploring. Often you can set up tents and camp ashore overnight, adding a whole new dimension to your cruising.

If you're a cruising couple, you can enjoy a degree of privacy unavailable to large coastal cruising yachts. You can sneak into tiny coves and inlets too shallow for deeper boats and have them all to yourselves. Here's your chance for a naked moonlight plunge without entertaining a whole fleet of nosy neighbors. You can trailer your boat to places off the beaten path and away from the crowds, find an unoccupied island and play Adam and Eve for an afternoon—or a weekend. If you're young and money comes hard, you're in luck. You won't need too much and you can do it now while you have energy and freedom of movement to take best advantage of what small boat cruising has to offer.

Here are some sample cruising plans you could do, depending on where you live:

1. You're a family of four living in Albany, N.Y. In the spring, you trailer your used 22-foot family weekender to a marina on beautiful Lake Champlain. You bought the boat in 1983 for $5000. Off and on during the summer you drive up to your boat, safely stored ashore at a marina, launch it at the marina's ramp, and go sailing. After your weekend cruise is finished, you haul the boat out again, park it ashore and drive back to Albany. You aren't hauling it around all the time; Lake Champlain is easily big enough to keep you interested all summer, and you've saved the cost of a slip or a mooring by launching the boat only when you need it. In the fall, you haul the boat back home and store it for free in your back yard. Next year maybe you'll do the same thing on Lake George, or on Lake Ontario, or on the Hudson.

2. You're a doctor, living on Long Island. Each year, your family enjoys swimming at your family cottage on the sound. You've purchased a 16-foot sloop, new for $4,200, and moored it a few dozen yards offshore. The boat has a small cabin with two bunks and a portable toilet. Most of the time you daysail the boat and use the cabin for changing in and out of bathing suits, going to the bathroom and as a safe playpen for visiting friends with small children. You and your wife have snuck out overnight a few times. Once, even though it was cramped in the cabin, you made love in there and then went for a midnight swim. You felt like kids again. Speaking of kids, your two boys have been campaigning to get your consent . . . They want to go on a week's cruise to Mystic, Connecticut and back. They are 16 and 13 and they're good sailors. The little boat seems safe enough and they really want to do it. You think maybe the next time they ask, you'll say yes.

3. You're a young couple in Phoenix, Arizona. You've only been married a year and, though you're both working, money is scarce. You've found a used cabin sloop only 14 feet long for $3,200. It has a reputation for making voyages of impressive distances and the two of you are intrigued. Your wife used to go canoeing and both of you are experienced backpackers.

After a season of happy sailing on some of the nearby desert lakes, you're planning trips to the Sea of Cortez. If that goes well, you might even take a year off work and sail the Gulf of Mexico from Mexico to Florida, exploring and occasionally working odd jobs along the way. Your parents think you're both nuts but you know you're not.

4. You're retired and living with your wife in Florida. You've always loved sailing and have owned several boats over the years from 27 to 41 feet. Now you want something very light and simple. Several companies not far from you manufacture boats about 17 feet long with comfortable berths and room for a modest galley that cost between $6–8,000.

Your kids, remembering the luxury of your earlier boats, can't picture you in something so compact. They think you're crazy, but you know you're not.

5. You're a student at the University of Oregon. You and two of your fraternity brothers have fixed up an old fishing dory and you're planning to spend the summer sailing and camping around Vancouver Island. You each have solo tents and backpacks. You figure the trip will cost $300 apiece—maximum. The boat cost you $100.

6. At a boat show last winter, you fell in love with a 16-foot sailboat

and surprised your family by driving home with it. Your wife is unmoved by your excuse that it was a steal at the boat show price. Now you're sitting with everybody at the dining room table with a road atlas spread out. You're circling all the places you can go cruising with a magic marker. You were beginning to agree with your wife that you had made a very costly mistake, but no longer. There are bunches of places to go sailing within driving distance of your house. Your kids are excited; your wife is slowly coming around, too. This is going to be even more fun than you thought.

A working family, a professional man, two newlyweds, a retired couple, three college students . . . all of them can enjoy most of the same pleasures as an affluent yachtsman:

Freedom: An escape from the ordinary world, the opportunity to follow the wind and leave your wristwatch at home.

Adventure: The thrill of exploring new places, experiencing the unexpected and taking as many personal risks as you are willing to take.

Romance: The visceral joy of a tanned body, warm water, sunsets, waves lapping against the hull . . .

Luxury: Here you and the yachtsman part company. For him, boating means pressurized water, electric lights—maybe even a shower on board—and a mortgage as hefty as the one on your home. For you, it means a warm place to lie down, a camp stove, a bath in the water you sail in, new cruising waters every time if you want, minimum financial investment, little risk and no worry.

Freedom, adventure, romance, these can all be yours if you can do without the luxury, once you stop thinking of your boat as a status symbol and start thinking of it instead as a ticket to freedom.

WHO OWNS WHAT?

In a meadow in Fairhaven, Massachusetts, lies the hull of a 27-foot sailboat. It's one of those kit jobs you can buy with the fiberglass hull already completed. All its owner had to do was build the plywood interior, rig mast and sails and go. It's half-finished and the man is exhausted, sick of it. He's put much more time and money into the job than he expected and he can't go on. He also can't get out. If he sells the boat as is, he'll lose his shirt. If he hires someone else to finish it, he'll have to ask more than it'll be worth. He doesn't have the boat, the boat has him.

A boyhood chum of mine and his wife went sailing on my 14-foot West Wight Potter. They loved it. A year later I had moved up to a 22-footer and after a weekend aboard that boat, they were hooked. They bought a 33-foot Hunter, convinced they could defray the boat's expenses by chartering it. My friend is an astute businessman and so he's off to a good start.

We went sailing the first summer on their new acquisition. The big boat absorbed five adults and a child with ease. Here was a boat you could really *live* on! But the previous charter customer had left the pressure on in the alcohol stove and when my friend leaned against it, it swung on its gimbals and dumped an astonishing quantity of explosive fuel onto the cabin sole. Then the first mate forgot to turn the pressure off on the head and soon water was flooding the toilet compartment.

Finally we got under way and, with our enormous draft, had to motor up the channel for the best part of an hour while all around us smaller sailboats zoomed around wherever they liked.

This year my friend is tired. His wife is getting sick of hearing about boats and he's sick of not being able to sail. Suddenly his pride and joy has become a trap. If he lowered his boat into one of the local Pennsylvania lakes, the water level would probably rise three inches. If he just sailed the boat and forgot the charter business, he'd go broke. If he chartered it all season long, he'd turn a small profit and he'd also go nuts. He doesn't have the boat any more, it has him.

What's going on here? My friend himself summed it up: "I forgot what it was I really wanted. I really wanted to go sailing, to be on the water, to go to sleep hearing the waves lap against the hull. But I got distracted. I started comparing boats and got involved in all the features these boats had. I started falling in love with *boats* instead of with sailing."

There's a funny paradox here. Certainly you can't go sailing without a boat, yet if you start thinking more about the *object* than you do about the *activity*, something starts to go wrong. You become a materialist.

Your spouse, with an unerring nose for trouble, begins to hate the boat and its intrusion into your heart.

"How can anyone be jealous of a thing?" you ask. "Easily," I reply, as one who knows. We fall very easily into love with things. It's not good for us.

Here's my advice; it's the underlying premise of this book: Think minimum. Buy something that costs less than you can afford. Accept the challenge. Find ways to make do. Don't borrow money for it. Don't get anxious about it. Keep it fun. J. P. Morgan was correct when he said, "If you have to ask how much it is, you can't afford it." Arrogant, but right. By all means go sailing. Escape to the thousands of rivers and lakes and bays and estuaries and ocean beaches this country and its neighbors have to offer. Swim, sail, let your boat drift and feel the sun on your body; camp aboard or ashore and sleep under the stars. Explore a different waterway every time you go out. But keep it simple. Don't overinvest. Mountain climbers carry all their needs on their backs. Why should you need more? Go sailing. Then, when you return, park your boat in your garage or in the back yard and forget it until you're ready to go somewhere in it again. Being able to forget your boat is important. That's how you'll know it's your property, that it belongs to you, not you to it. I love sailing but I have only recently learned wisdom.

WHAT WILL IT COST?

When I was a boy, my family sailed around the Chesapeake in a big steel cutter we'd built ourselves. My father did the lion's share of the heavy work on her. One year, when we got a temporary break in the winter weather, we drove on down from Philadelphia to have a visit with it. The steel hull was immune to damage from the kind of ice Maryland's Eastern Shore usually dished out, so we had covered the boat with a canvas tarp and left her in the water. Dad had given the yard a list of

odd jobs to do about the boat and, month by month through the winter, bills for this and that had been coming in. I guess it seemed reasonable on this warm afternoon to drive down and see how things were progressing.

After a three-hour drive, my father arrived to find the tarp still tied in place and the boat untouched since October. Needless to say, he was annoyed and took the issue up with the owner of the yard, a venerable figure in my memory—designer, boat builder, someone I had liked. During the ensuing discussion, such things were pointed out as the realities of cash flow over the winter season and the yard's every intention to perform all the agreed-on tasks. The old gentleman finished up the discussion like this:

"Mr. Brown," he said, "boating is a very expensive hobby. If you can't keep up with it, perhaps you should consider golf or tennis or some other less expensive form of recreation."

My anger and frustration return to me fresh whenever I recall that conversation. My parents always worked hard. My father has worked relentlessly as long as I can remember, but we never were able to go sailing—or do anything else for that matter—as though we were indifferent to the cost. I was stunned by the arrogance of the man to suggest that if we couldn't go effortlessly, we shouldn't go.

For the record, we switched boat yards, smashing a gratifying path through the Choptank River ice in the process. I'd like to return, for the moment, to the yardmaster's premise: that if we can't go effortlessly, we shouldn't go. I couldn't disagree with that more profoundly. If the sea "belongs" to anyone, it is to those who love it, rich *or* poor. I'm going

SAILING ON A MICRO-BUDGET

. . . and forget about it. (PHOTOS BY C. KING)

to assume, dear reader, that you, like me, can't go effortlessly, as though you were indifferent to the cost. So let's take a look at the cost of owning a boat. I've developed an obsession on the subject, even kept records on boat prices going back over the last decade. You can't keep records for 10 years without noticing things; what do they show?:

1. Although boats are sold on the basis of their length, you really pay for them by the pound. Obviously, a boat with expensive fittings and fine cabinetry will cost more, but basically when you buy a fiberglass boat, *you're buying fiberglass by the pound.* At the time of this writing in 1984, plastic yachts cost $5 a pound. In 1980, they cost $4 a pound. In 1974, 10 years ago, they cost slightly less than $3. At first blush, this will seem to be a gross oversimplification, but if you chart out the latest price of sailboats based on their weight, you'll see an almost linear relationship. There is one discrepancy worth noting here: the smallest sailboats, those about 20 feet and under, or those weighing less than 1,800 pounds, tend to cost more, about $6–$7 a pound. Why? Remember that even if the boat is very small, there are still manufacturing stages that must be gone through. In terms of *labor,* small boats are less efficient to build than larger ones. Manufacturers would naturally rather sell a few big boats than lots of little ones—a good reason why the joys of small boat cruising are not pitched too hard.

In the last 10 years, sailboat costs have increased approximately 250 percent. The rate of increase has been a fairly constant 12 percent a year and will most likely continue that way. There is a great temptation for manufacturers to try making their boats lighter. If they can save on fiberglass, they can still bump their prices along every year and increase

The Invitation

their profits at the same time. It's interesting to save old brochures from manufacturers to see the pounds slipping away.

2. Here's another way you can look at it. Sailboats, on the average, tend to double in weight and in cost with every five-foot increment in length. A 20-footer will cost twice as much as a 15-footer, a 25 twice as much as a 20-footer and so on. Size is expensive. Remember: every dollar you *don't* spend on your boat is available for something else, travel for example.

THE DOUBLING RULE OF FIVES

Average 15-footer	$3,000– $4,600
Average 20-footer	$6,000– $8,000 & up
Average 25-footer	$14,000–$17,000 & up
Average 30-footer	$28,000–$44,000 & up

---

3. The cost of buying a boat is further magnified when you buy it on time. The installment plan tempts you to buy a bigger boat than you need, especially when the salesman *wants* you to buy a higher-ticket item. Look what happens to you when you buy on time. These are the prices at a major New England boat dealership in 1980. Bank rates fluctuate continually, but the exercise is instructive.

THE BOAT	Its list price 1980	Total paid including interest payments	Years of loan payments	Interest paid out	With the interest you could have bought:
Macgregor 21	$5,680	$7,325	5 years	$1,660	Two wind surfers
Edel 18	$7,400	$9,500	5 years	$2,150	A Hobie 14 catamaran
Chrysler 22	$9,700	$13,900	7 years	$3,200	A 15′ West Wight Potter
Chrysler 26	$15,300	$24,800	10 years	$9,500	A Chrysler 22
Hunter 27	$26,150	$44,500	11 years	$18,300	A Chrysler 26 (for 1 more foot!)
Hunter 30	$35,700	$63,100	12 years	$27,400	A Hunter 27

If you can possibly avoid buying on time, avoid it. Start very small and pay cash. Buy a used daysailer and have fun with it for a few years while you save up. Take it places where you can camp along shore. Rig a boom tent and sleep in the cockpit, but stay out of the installment racket. How do you think the bank president affords his nice yacht?

4. The money you spend in monthly payments will end up coming out of your entertainment and/or vacation budget. The ultimate object of owning a boat is not owning a boat, it is doing something in it. Think small. Pay cash. The only nice thing I can say looking back over the boats I have owned and financed is that I made enough interesting mistakes to write a book about it.

SAILING ON A MICRO-BUDGET

5. Let's go through an exercise to see how little it really does cost to go sailing on a small boat. It's crucial to understand that fiberglass boats don't deteriorate. So, the well-maintained boat and trailer you buy today for $5,000, is likely to retain a minimum of 75% of its value (whether bought new or used) three years from today. If that's so, then today's $5,000 boat will be worth at least $3,750 in three years. Your out-of-pocket loss in depreciation during that time will be $417 a year. Let's add to that some of the other costs of ownership and sailing:

$ 417	Depreciation
100	Insurance
125	Maintenance
50	Registration fees
125	Gasoline to get your boat where you want to vacation
500	Food and supplies two weeks summer cruise
500	Food and supplies two weeks winter cruise
$1812	
÷ 365	
$4.96 a day!	

BUYING USED BOATS

Given the general national trend of boat buyers to purchase a new and bigger boat every few years, there is a brisk trade in used small boats. It's a good suggestion, if you're new to boating, to have a boat inspected before you buy it. A local dealer, for a few bucks, may have one of his workmen come down to look at a used boat with you if you're really interested.

A used boat often comes equipped with compass, anchor, line, trailer, even occasionally such exotica as depth sounder or radio direction finder. For what you'd pay for a new boat, you can get a good used one *with trailer* and loaded with goodies. Sometimes you can produce a thick pile of folding green and offer to pay cash *right now* and get the boat for much less than the seller listed it for—especially if he's desperate to sell. If you're really short on money, this may be the only way to get a boat. Just keep looking and trying.

OTHER COSTS OF OWNERSHIP

Now the good news: The costs of owning and maintaining a small boat are very low. You usually can store your boat in the backyard for nothing. If you trailer your boat, you won't be leaving it in the water and can skip mooring or slip fees at a marina. Bottom paint can cost $60. a gallon, but you won't need any if you store your boat ashore.

Insurance on my 15-foot Potter costs about $100. a year. If you plan to travel with your boat, make sure you are covered for *all* the waters you plan to sail in. It costs more to do that but the expense is worthwhile. Imagine having an accident far from home and then discovering, upon your return, that you were not covered.

Fees go up sharply with the value of your boat. Many experienced sailors who live aboard their boats sail uninsured to escape the expense. For the best deal, contact the people who insure your car and get them to cover your boat and its trailer as well. They'll often give you a lower rate as a courtesy, if they already cover your house or car. Shop around to make sure you're getting the best price.

A SAILING EXPEDITION

You're planning for your two-week vacation. You've got the spot picked out—a big lake about 300 miles from where you live. What's this going to cost?

1. Obviously you've got gas out and back. Add 25 percent for excursions.
2. Let's assume you've got space in your boat and in your car, wagon or van to bed down everybody in your family. Maybe you have tents, too, though you can't use them everywhere. (You can pull over at a highway rest area for the night but you can't pitch a tent there.) If you've got a bed for everybody, then you won't have the expense of motels to worry about. Budget one night's worth, though, just in case you have a period of rain and morale gets low.
3. Rough out menus for the time you'll be gone. From that you can calculate your food budget. Find out what it costs to feed your family at MacDonalds® and assume you'll eat out one meal in four. I know, you've promised yourselves that this time you won't do that, but you will. It's vacation. Budget it in.
4. Add up gas, food, and lodging . . . then add 50 percent. "What for?" you ask. "We've been so scientific up till now." Damned if I know. All I know is we run out of money every year and never do anything noticeably stupid. I don't know where it goes; it just goes. Take half as much clothes and twice as much money and you'll be fine. Trust me.

A FINAL THOUGHT

What does sailing really cost? Look at it this way. Divide the cost of your boat per year by the days of sailing you get in. That's what it costs.

There are two ways you can improve on this picture: spend less; sail more. If you want to do both of those things, *get a small boat*. You'll obviously spend less. Less obviously but equally important, you'll use the boat more. Taking off spontaneously on a breezy afternoon to a nearby river or lake will seem less intimidating, more worth doing. You'll do more daysailing. If you're driving somewhere interesting, you can drag your boat along without much bother and even use it as a trailer overnight should you decide to linger. And should a pretty lake appear along your route. . . .

One final advantage of a small boat: you will spend less time trying to figure out what it costs when you're absolutely certain you can afford it.

LIFE ABOARD

PART II

On small boats, you'll do most of your cooking in the cockpit. On *really* small boats, there's no other place.

BASIC CONCERNS

Now the crucial part. How can we accomplish in a small boat all the necessary life-support functions: cooking, sleeping, keeping clean, and storing clothes and gear? Before we deal with each of these, let's remember the mountain climber again, the one carrying everything he needs on his back. Think minimum. If you do, you *can* make everything fit.

Food and Cooking

We Americans are strange creatures. Before we eat almost anything, we either warm it up or cool it off. Room temperature, evidently, is a bore. That's a pity because it would be so much easier on our insides if we weren't creatures of such extremes.

If we could do without an ice chest, we would save lots of space and annoyance. Beer, soda and water can be kept reasonably cool stored in the bilge. Dairy products, on the other hand, especially milk, spoil rapidly if not kept cold. Milk is useful mostly for cereal in the morning. It's a hard meal to pass up because cereal is so quick and easy to fix and so filling. Try out the instant and canned varieties of milk. If cereal tastes all right that way, you've got it made. If not, you can either drop cereal from your menu or buy the smallest available cooler to just keep a ½-gallon of milk cold. Solid ice, by the way, lasts much longer than cubes. On a bigger boat, try a 2-icebox system. Meat and other things that don't need to be available except at mealtimes are kept in the never-opened master chest, stored someplace out of the way. Keep a small second cooler for juice, etc. (well-rationed) handy. This, of course, if you *must* have an icebox.

If you can do without ice, you probably won't want to do without a stove. A hot meal is good for morale. Many foods simply cannot be prepared without cooking.

From all the scare stories I've heard and read, I'd avoid alcohol stoves. The *un*pressurized varieties that require no pumping or priming are certainly safer but any flammable liquid fuel stored in a small boat is a hazard to be avoided.

Life Aboard

On the right hand side of the cabin, the slide-out galley of the Catalina 22. Such a rig only intrudes into the cabin area when you want it . . . otherwise it stows under the cockpit seat. On the left, a dinette/double berth arrangement.

A homemade galley installed in a MacGregor 22. Note silverware rack on aft end, a fold up table, sink stuffed with dishes, propane stove. Sink and stove lift for access to storage below.

Sterno is simple and very safe but the flame isn't hot enough for some cooking. You may not be able to make pancakes on a sterno stove. There is a good gimballed stove made for sterno but it's bulky and you may not have room for it in a really small boat.

Propane camping stoves are probably the best bet. They put out a good hot flame and some of them are very compact. We have a single burner propane stove and a simple sterno stove as a back up for low heat cooking—like soup. It's a good idea to have a portable galley to set up in the cockpit or to take ashore for camping.

Eggs actually keep at room temperature for quite a while. Liquid margarine in a squeeze bottle keeps nicely, too. It's good for frying or on sandwiches. Fruit, lettuce, tomatoes, onions, carrots, all keep well for a few days. Rice, dried grains and beans, of course, are ideal.

Camping supply places often stack supplies of freeze-dried meals that are light and compact. Supermarkets have soup, stew and hot cereals in freeze-dried packets. Try these out at home and see what you like.

Of course, there's always canned food. It stores well in little out-of-the-way places; it keeps, and some of it even tastes pretty good. Again, while ashore, have one "can night" a week and try things out.

Make up daily menus in advance, before you leave. Try packaging the contents of each meal in "zip-lock"-type bags and label each bag. Everything you can do at home, do at home.

Finally, try packing everything into two open plastic laundry baskets. Check for fit under your quarter berths or wherever you have space. Put pots, pans, cutting board, dishes and mugs (mugs can serve as bowls), can openers, matches, silverware, spatula, and stove in one basket, food in the other. Pack all food into plastic bags or watertight containers. Carry a plastic bag or two for trash. Now you're all set. What you've got is easy to get into and out of the car and into and out of the boat. On a bigger boat, you may eventually build in a galley but with this system, you may not want to bother.

Sanitation

If you're in fresh water, keeping clean is usually as simple as falling overboard with a cake of biodegradable soap. If you're in salt water, you can get clean but you still have to get the salt off. Salt permeates clothes and bedding and attracts moisture. Soon everything begins to feel clammy. A solar shower is a simple way to rinse off. A stingy way to rinse off with a limited supply of fresh water is to take a sponge bath, starting at your head and working down. The cockpit floor is an ideal and semi-private place to bathe.

Dishes can be washed in shallow plastic pans. A pan for soapy water and a pan for fresh makes sense. When you wash in cool water—especially if it's cool salt water—you need all the help you can get. Teflon pans help. For dishes as well as for you, use a biodegradable shampoo.

Finally we come to everyone's favorite, the marine toilet. Coast Guard regulations forbid toilets that discharge wastes over the side. I find it strange that yachtsmen, who claim to love the sea, take such perverse pride in flouting the intent of this law. The law is worded in such a way that it *is* legal to go sailing with *no* toilet. Many sailors carry a sweet-smelling cedar bucket and operate on a "bucket and chuck it" philoso-

The portable toilet. Some simple models cost less than $30.

phy. After all, it's not illegal to have a bucket that discharges over the side. Let others do as they like, sailors should be the most untiring advocates of marine ecology. We should, therefore, take care not to foul the waters we sail and swim in. I grant you, sometimes you will take your porta-potty ashore and empty it in a marina toilet only to flush it back, via municipal sewage pipes, to the waterway. Shame on them, then. Get the town to clean up its act. If we finally succeed in poisoning our oceans, the jig will really be up. So forget about cedar buckets and get a portable head.

On boats from 17 feet and up, there's usually a convenient spot ready-made for a marine head. On many smaller boats, especially centerboard boats, there isn't a convenient spot for the thing and when you move into the cabin at night, it moves out into the cockpit. You wouldn't want it next to your nose anyway.

Actually, portable heads are OK if you empty the holding tank periodically and add the deodorant. The inexpensive ones have one drawback. They're flexible. When you sit on them, they squash just a bit, and when they squash, they exhale a puff of vapor from their holding tank. That's why you want to change the tank often and not allow it to ferment in your boat for a week or two between voyages. If you have space on your boat for a larger, more heavily built potty and can afford one, you'd be well advised to make the investment. On long car trips, the portable toilet can be handy if rest stop locations are few and far between. Here also, the cedar bucket just won't do.

Sleeping

Go lie down somewhere, just to see how much room you need. Don't just lie there at attention, be natural. Now measure. Length, for some reason, is more critical than width. You need room for your feet to extend when you lie on your stomach. A narrow berth is manageable if you're wedged into it but it's hell if you're falling off one edge all the time. Many small boats offer berths that require a filler cushion placed between them to gain a comfortable width. Sometimes flotation cushions or seabags can fill in the gap. Before you go on your first cruise, try taking a nap aboard, even while the boat's in your back yard. You'll learn a lot that way.

You've got to keep your bunks dry. That's hard on a small boat with kids in wet bathing suits crawling around. Large trash bags pulled over the after part of the cushions will shed water during the day and can be pulled off at night. Sleeping bags can be stored in heavy duty trash bags by day if there's a chance spray or wet children will soak them.

Try inflatable camping pillows covered with regular pillow cases. Don't inflate them too much. If you like them, leave your house pillows at home. If inflatable mattresses fit in your boat, use them. They can't get soaked through and they provide additional flotation in an emergency.

Unless you have a big boat and adequate storage, don't bring sheets. On warm nights why not sleep naked or wear light clothing? It's best to keep one set of warm sleep gear separate and never ever use it for anything else. That way you're sure to have something dry when you go to bed.

So here you are, your very first night on your new boat, bobbing at anchor. You and your wife are snuggled into bed. It's cozy. You both grin. Through the open hatchway you see stars coming out. This is going to be neat. Soon your wife's regular breathing tells you she's asleep. You notice a slight pressure on your bladder and speculate idly whether you'll last the night without having to visit the head. Considering that and other imponderable questions, you drift off to sleep.

You're awakened suddenly by a loud bump. You note the wind has risen and the boat is zigging and zagging around at anchor. The sail you had carelessly furled last night has partially come loose and it's flapping

The generous vee berth of the Montgomery 15 with the head stored away under the filler cushion. This keel/centerboarder also offers a small footwell for sitting comfort.

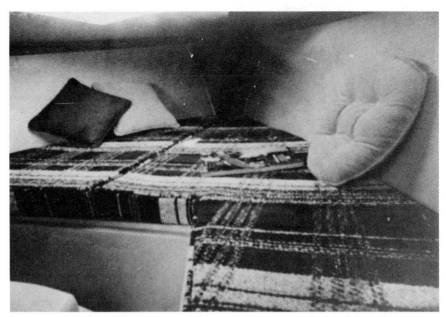

The vee berth in larger boats, like this Catalina 22, is an ideal spot for kids. In some boats, the berths are too small for taller adults, anyway.

restlessly. It's so warm in your sleeping bag, you decide to ignore it all and wait till morning. For some reason, however, you're suddenly attuned to each and every sound, however subtle. Somewhere in the distance, someone's dog barks. The bump returns—but only once. You glance at your wife and she's blissfully asleep! A gust of wind makes the boat tremble. Looking out the window, you realize with panic that the view is totally unlike the one you went asleep to. *By God, you're adrift!* You spring to action and are in the cockpit in a trice. It's colder than you could believe for the time of year and wet, too. Your bare feet are wet and cold. Looking around, you realize the wind has shifted. You're still in the same place, just facing a different way. Feeling your wet way carefully along the cabin top, you gather in the sail and tie it down. Your foot slips and you sit your bare fanny down on the cabin roof. The voice of your wife comes to you through the hatch. "You all right?"

Back in your bunk, teeth chattering, feet throbbing with cold, you find your wife has taken you at your word and is again fast asleep. You settle in and, at this point, realize you won't make it to morning without returning to the cockpit to use the head. . . .

Before turning in for the night, check around the boat for things that make noise. If the halyards ping against the mast when the night breeze gets up, tie them out to the shrouds to get them away from the mast. When I was a boy, I remember being lulled to sleep by the slow soft slap of halyards against the tall wooden masts of the vessels we used to sail. The nervous ping-ping-ping of nylon on aluminum has taken all the romance out of it.

If your centerboard is down, it may bump back and forth in its trunk. If your mast is loosely stayed, it too may thrash around. Tie your tiller amidships so it won't bump. Finally, check your anchor to reassure yourself that it's holding securely. Check your surroundings carefully so you'll be able to tell if you've drifted. There. Now you can get some sleep.

For all your best precautions, don't be discouraged if your first night out you sleep poorly. After years of sailing, my first night on each trip is often fitful. There are sounds to get used to and my instinct is to consider each noise and satisfy my mind that I know what it represents. Then there are stars. Nights on the water, especially moonlit ones, are so beautiful that I can often lie awake for hour after hour just soaking it in. I remember doing so as a boy. We have forgotten such things, living as we do, and when we find them again we are stunned, almost in disbelief.

Even if you do lose some sleep the first night out, later nights make up for it. After a few days of getting up with the sun and going down with the sun, I am sleeping with a soundness and waking with a wholeness I rarely find on land.

Stowing Your Gear

The usual weekend sailor packs everything into a cylindrical canvas seabag. This is tossed onto a bunk later on. There are two things about seabags: They take up space where someone might sit or lie down, and no matter how you pack, the thing you want is always on the bottom. The smaller your boat, the more urgent it is you do away with seabags. The secret is to hang the inside walls of your cabin with monkey hammocks and thin canvas pouches. Give everyone one monkey hammock and one canvas pouch. Sleeping bags can be rolled tight and tucked against the cabin sides; pillows can be stuffed out of the way in the peak. If you can keep the bunks clear for sitting or sleeping, you can cruise in comfort—even in a tiny boat.

The cabin of a popular compact cruiser, the MacGregor 21. Here's the challenge: How do you set this boat up for cruising? Where will you put the toilet, a stove, food supplies, your clothes and yourselves. It's entirely possible—even on boats much smaller.

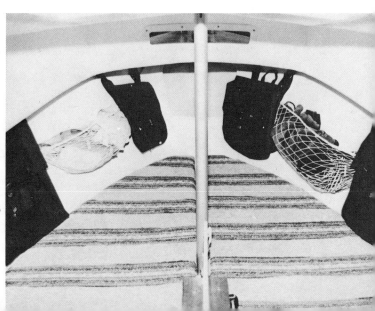

Here's the first step—a vital one—to moving in. Hang the sides of the boat with monkey hammocks, pouches, wicker baskets, whatever works. Get your stuff off the bunks and floor so you can actually crawl in and lie down if you want to.

It takes practice to get your gear down to the bare essentials. Make it a habit always to check after each trip to see what you used or wore and what you didn't. Next time leave home everything you did without. In terms of clothing, here's a suggested list of what to bring:

One pair of swim trunks. This'll probably be your basic wardrobe. Tank suits double nicely as undergarments, since they're easy to wash and dry in a flash.

One pair of comfortable shorts. Try to keep these reasonably dry. You'll live in these.

(for men) *One pair of underpants.* They'll feel great after your first shoreside shower before going out for a seafood feast.

One pair of comfortable long pants. These should be light color (preferably white) and of a fabric that dries quickly. In cooler weather take those pants your wife wants to throw out but you love too much to let her.

An old white shirt. After you've gotten sunburned, you'll wear this. Get it wet to cool it off on hot days—even jump in with it on.

Two pair white socks —one to wear after your feet and shins get sunburned, one civilized pair to wear ashore.

A comfortable, very loose-hooded sweatshirt. It's for sleeping. Get one two sizes too big. The loose hood can be pulled down over your eyes to keep the early morning sun from waking you up.

A really warm wool sweater. The one you're embarrassed to wear in public anymore will do fine.

A floppy hat. Get a white one. This will shade your eyes and the back of your neck. Soak the hat from time to time in hot water to keep your head cool.

A pair of sunglasses and a pair of clip-on sunglasses. If you're sailing west at sundown you may need both at once to cut down the glare. The sun reflecting off the water, off white fiberglass decks and off the sails can give you a headache and even can damage your eyes.

One pair of really beat up sneakers for going wading when the bottom is rocky or strewn with broken shells or glass.

One pair of presentable sneakers to wear when the grubby pair is wet or for wearing ashore.

A Lacoste shirt and white shorts for cutting a yachty figure ashore or for looking appealing enough to convince some seaside facility to let you tie up at their dock overnight.

A cheap set of $3.00 rain top and pants. The top doubles as a windbreaker. Discount stores sell these. Foul weather gear is for yachts. Disposable kinds fold up into a tiny pouch and take up no space. If it's a warm rain, just wear your bathing suit.

That's about all the clothes you'll need on most summer cruises. Just remember that the ultimate purpose of cruising is to be out on the water and to see new places. I've often brought so much stuff I had little room left to turn around. I can't remember when I've been out cruising and wished I had more clothes.

Many boats have cockpit storage bins called lazarettes. These are marvelous for storing fenders and life jackets. If your boat doesn't have one, you can hang things on hooks from the inside of your transom. Oars can be fitted through the oarlocks and tied to the stern cleats so they won't fall out. You can drill small holes in the blades of oars to facilitate tying them down. You also can tie oars to the shrouds or figure some way to attach them to the mast. In either of those places, they may slam around while you're rocking at anchor and keep you awake.

A bow pulpit is a good idea. Not only is it a safety feature for kids, who love being up in the bow, it's a perfect perch for your anchor and line. Stern pulpits also are ideal for hanging gear out of the way as well as welcome things to lean up against.

Always remember that the worst place for anything is on the floor or lying on the bunks. A mess on a small boat is bad for morale and it's dangerous if anyone has to move around in a hurry.

One last suggestion. Designate certain clothes as "boat stuff" and keep it on board in the monkey hammocks. You might need to launder it when you get home, but store it all aboard. Store some old pots and pans aboard, too. Then, when the mood strikes you, grab some food and go. Just like that. Knowing you can run off and go sailing whenever the mood strikes you is the greatest comfort of all.

Bringing Pets Aboard

When I was a boy, we used to sail with our Siamese cat. Of course, we were sailing a big catboat so his presence aboard was a visual pun, so to speak. It was a wooden boat, so when the cat got unnerved, he could dig his claws into the deck (or wherever he happened to be) for a foothold. I'm sure he went to the bathroom somehow, but I have forgotten the details.

Cats have been traditional crew on ships for a very long time. They catch mice, are quiet, clean, surefooted and reasonably small. I had a seagoing cat a few years ago, Magellan. He went riding on my first Potter and seemed to like it, at first. During our first cruise in rough weather, Magellan found he couldn't get a clawhold into fiberglass. He lost his balance while up on the cabin top and tumbled off into the cockpit. Cats have an innate sense of dignity and Magellan didn't appreciate the loss of his. He retired to the inner recesses of the cabin to think things over. That night, we tied up in Woods Hole next to a 50-foot steel fishing boat. The boat had an enormous woman aboard who made a big fuss over him. Later that night, the wind shifted and we got the full aroma of our neighbor's cargo. That must have been more than Magellan could stand. By morning, the screen on the main hatch was pushed out and our cat was gone. So was the fishing boat. I imagine Magellan is rolling in ecstasy in the bilges of what must seem to him a 50-foot can of cat food. He must weigh 30 pounds by now.

I sailed out of Woods Hole feeling abandoned and lonely. Since the morning Magellan jumped ship, I haven't taken another pet sailing, nor do I expect to.

Pets are fun, but on the water you have these problems: They fall overboard; they get stepped on; they get frightened and moan piteously,

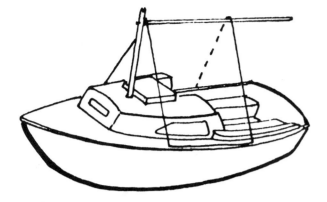

HATCHWAY TENT

This is the simplest there is. It covers half the cockpit and the hatchway. You can get into and out of the cabin in the rain and have a dry spot outside the cabin for the head.

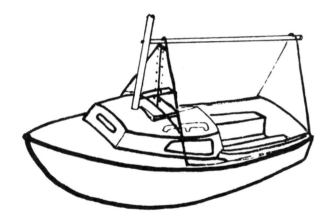

FULL COCKPIT BOOM TENT

Obviously you get better protection. Takes up more space to stow. Harder to get into and out of the boat. Sitting in the cockpit is cramped. Modern short booms will still expose the aft cockpit to rainfall.

"CONESTOGA WAGON" COVER

Variations of this approach can turn your cockpit into another much bigger cabin. Sitting is dry and comfortable. The "conestoga" cover would be the most bulky to store, the most elaborate to set up, and would offer the most windage if a squall came up.

demoralizing the children. Furthermore pets both eat and go to the bathroom, both of which, especially the latter, are a real problem on a small boat. A cat's box is hell to live with in a space the size of a phone booth. If you heel way over and distribute the contents of that box into the secret recesses of your bilge, you may as well burn your boat.

Dogs are worse, making much more noise and requiring not only food but regular walks ashore. People with big powerboats (you know the kind with flying bridges and acres of plate glass) often keep dogs. They're always poodles. I met a couple living aboard a small sailboat with their German shepard. I remember seeing the two of them rowing ashore with this huge black dog wobbling precariously in the bow of the dinghy.

Someday when I become rich and famous maybe I'll have a really big boat with one stateroom just for pets. The floor will be lined with newspapers and I'll put an exhaust fan in each porthole. Until then my animals will stay ashore.

USING THE COCKPIT

The smaller your boat, the more vital it is to tent over your cockpit and make use of its space. If the cabin of a small boat is your boudoir, the cockpit is your living room and kitchen all rolled into one. If your boat only has two berths and if your crew consists of more than two, then you have another reason to come up with a reliable rain cover. People have to sleep out there. The first order of business is to contrive a wooden cockpit floor that can be raised level with the seats. That creates a nice double bunk.

Boom Tents

The simplest shelter solution is to make up a boom tent. All you need is a waterproof tarp that can be draped over the boom and snapped or tied in place outside the cockpit coaming. The tent should also cover the entire hatchway and should preferably have end flaps to keep wind-driven rain out. The one drawback of boom tents is the sides slope abruptly and leave little room to sit up in the seats. Still, they are the least expensive and simplest option available.

A simple boom tent converts this Leeward 16, an open day sailer with a cuddy, into a snug overnighter. (PHOTO BY LUGER INDUSTRIES)

Here's going in style! The Siren 17 offers this elaborate cockpit shelter that turns the whole area into a dry, well-lit extension of the cabin. It's not inexpensive, but costs a lot less than a bigger boat. (PHOTO BY VANDESTADT & MCGRUER)

Bimini Tops

A more elegant and flexible system is the Bimini top. The Bimini top folds down over the cabin top when not in use, then pops up to shelter the cockpit. Most boats can be rigged to sail with the Bimini top in place. Biminis provide marvelous sun protection. You'd need side panels to keep the rain out. They tend, however, to leak or blow open in strong winds. Bimini tops also are expensive. If you have inside provisions for the whole crew, the Bimini top would be a wonderful luxury—even a necessity in southern latitudes.

The generous Bimini top on The Tramp trimaran.

Dodgers cover only the hatchway and the after end of the cabin. They shield the cockpit from flying spray and, in rainy weather, allow you to leave the hatch open so you can get some air.

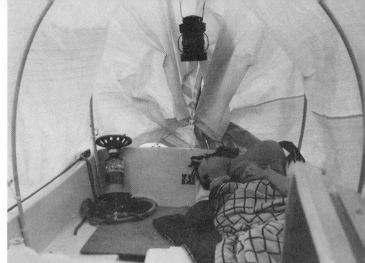

With a Conestoga cover, the enclosed cockpit is light and airy. The flexible plastic pipes stow inside the cabin when not in use.

A Conestoga cockpit cover maximizes the space on very small boats.

Conestoga Tops

A third option, standard on the Drascombe boats, custom built on anything else, is a free-standing "Conestoga wagon" affair using fiberglass wands or lengths of ½-inch plastic plumbing pipe. Three of these can be bent in graceful arcs to cover the cockpit and secured to the outside of the coaming. A tarp can be draped over top and tied down. Then one can sit normally in the cockpit seats without hunching over. With part of the tarp rolled back for visibility, the boat could even be sailed or motored that way, depending on the height of the shelter.

In one form or another, you'll gain enormous benefits from weatherproofing your cockpit. The cost of the covering, even a sophisticated one, is well below the cost of a larger boat. Maybe that's the best way to look at it.

Camping Ashore

Another highly enjoyable option is to purchase a camping tent, store it under the cockpit floor, and spend an occasional night ashore. If you own a truly beachable boat, this offers enormous flexibility. Of course the tent is available for overland camping trips, too. Some cruising areas are too populated to allow shoreside camping but tenting in wilderness areas is not only possible, it's delightful.

This Sea Pearl 21 is part of a shoreline campsite on the Florida coast.

Finally, don't forget hotels. If you're near seacoast or lakeside towns, budget yourself one night in a hotel. Then if it rains when you're already wet, if you've been hot all day and at 8:30 p.m. it's still 92° or if for any reason a night of luxury appeals to you, go for it. Tie up, lock up, and enjoy a long shower and night out in a strange port.

Some Good Reading:

More Boat Canvas: Topsides projects by Karen Lipe
  Seven Seas Press, Newport, RI

COMFORTING THOUGHTS

Being comfortable at sea consists primarily of the following:

- Being warm when it's cold
- Being cool when it's warm
- Keeping yourself and your things dry
- Keeping the bugs away

Keeping Warm

This may sound simplistic but we'll assume that you can always put on a sweater or a windbreaker when you're cold. A candle lantern in the cabin can take the edge off a cool night without suffocating you or subjecting you to the risk of spilled kerosene from one of those nautical lanterns. You can stick a flashlight to the cabin wall with Velcro for a multi-purpose light, but it sheds no warmth. Basically, as long as you can stay dry, you can probably stay warm.

Keeping Cool

Staying cool, especially in the tropics or in midsummer, is more of a problem. Most small production boats offer little ventilation, sometimes none. For moderate cost you can add air scoops to your foredeck or cabin top. They really help and, faced away from the wind, even work in the rain.

As we've already mentioned, Bimini tops give you the chance to sail in the shade. Especially if some of your family sunburn easily, this is important. The simple spray bottles sold to spray the leaves of house-plants can lay down a light cooling mist over your skin on a hot day. If you have tots on board, be careful they do not proceed, back home, to direct *other* sprays into their faces and onto their skins, expecting similar relief.

At the risk of looking like the good humor man, wear white. Wear thin, loose-fitting whites and spray your upper clothes with water and let the evaporation help cool you. Wearing a wet bandana around your head helps keep the sun off and keeps your head cool. Being bald I'm lost without one. Working the same principle, a damp towel can help keep the ice chest cool, too. Glare from water and white fiberglass can be severe. Bring sunglasses and a sun block lotion. Frequent swim stops are good for morale, too.

If your clothes should be white in hot weather, your towels should be dark—black, brown or navy blue. They'll dry a lot faster.

Keeping Dry

We've already discussed ways to keep your bedding dry by protecting mattresses and sleeping bags with plastic bags. While dodgers don't offer much sun protection, they shield the cockpit from flying spray and permit you to keep your hatch open while it's raining. Dodgers and Biminis offer you some of the comforts of bigger boats without the hassles and expense. Looked at that way, they're a bargain. They're much cheaper than a bigger boat.

Keeping Bugs Away

Even when everything else is perfect, bugs can ruin everything. There's a new electronic device coming on the market that's supposed to emit an ultra high frequency tone that bugs can't stand. If it works, get one for your cabin (and maybe one for your cockpit if your boat is that large) and disregard all further discussions about Velcro-attached screens and bug repellant. If you can't find one of these miracle devices or if you can't afford one, or if it proves ineffective, Velcro-attached screen kits are sold in most marine supply stores. I made up my own screens with Velcro, mosquito netting and a sewing machine. The folded screen doesn't take up space when not in use and you'll need it in many of the places you sail. Screening in a boom tent or Bimini top is a more expensive proposition. Still nothing beats sitting out in the cool of the evening and watching the sun go down knowing the little bastards can't get to you.

Remedies of last resort: take a prolonged swim at dusk and don't come out till it's safe. Get a spray can of bug repellant and use it liberally. A little bug repellant spray around the places where your screens snap or attach to the hull or to the Bimini top will discourage bugs from crawling through the chinks in your defenses.

LAUNCHING AND TRAILERING YOUR BOAT

Launching

If you're getting a portable boat, presumably you plan to launch it yourself from public boat ramps. The ease with which you can do this will determine how much, and how spontaneously, you use your boat.

If trailering is going to be a basic part of your sailing, then I urge you to get the smallest boat you think you can stand and to get a shallow draft, centerboard design. If the boat is easy to launch and retrieve, you won't hesitate to take off on a Saturday afternoon for a daysail. You'll have more fun. The critical measurement to look at, as you compare boats, is the boat's height from the roadway to the waterline as it sits on its trailer. That's about how deep you'll have to sink the boat/trailer before the boat will float free. The problem is that while you want to submerge the trailer, you *don't* want to submerge your car doing it. There's the rub. The larger your boat and the deeper its keel, the further

WAYS TO GO:

ON THE ROAD OVERNIGHT
4 people in a medium sized boat
2 people in a small boat
2 people in a small boat, 2 more in wagon van or tent.

+

ON THE WATER OVERNIGHT
4 people in a medium sized boat
2 people in a small boat (kids in cockpit)

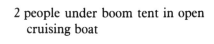

2 people under boom tent in open cruising boat

2 people in cabin
2 people in tent ashore

Burlington photographer Robert Doran happened by just in time to watch someone launch his truck. Some trailerable boats are more trailerable than others.

down the ramp you have to go to float it off. Soon you'll launch your car.

Some small boat trailers have a hinge that permits you to lift the bow into the air and slide the boat off into the water. Our Potter has one. It's so easy, it feels like you must be cheating somehow. Trailers with rollers make launching and retrieving easier still, especially with heavier, deeper hulls. Most of the boats we'll be discussing can be launched satisfactorily with stock trailers. I wouldn't spend extra money for rollers unless you tried the original equipment for a season and found it inadequate.

Our MacGregor 22, though it drew only 12 inches, was a much longer and heavier boat and more of a pain to launch, especially at boat ramps with very shallow inclines. We ended up connecting the trailer hitch to the trailer with a heavy 20-foot line. I'd give the trailer a shove over the edge of the incline, hop back into the van and then ease the rig down and into the water. That way I could float the boat off without even wetting my tires. Especially in salt water, that was a big plus. If you

Here's an ideal launching: You back down . . . give just a little push . . .

have a small keel boat, using a heavy line or chain might make life easier for you, too. Some companies make tongue extenders that offer the advantages of the line with superior control over the trailer.

Trailering

Most boats under 20 feet can be pulled easily by a compact family car. Boats weighing a ton or more will need the automotive power of a husky V-6 or a V-8 engine. Some people buy a big old gas guzzler just to tow their big sailboat. Ask the manufacturer of your car to specify its safe load limit.

Mounting a second trailer hitch on your *front* fender gives you superior visibility and control for launching and retrieving. This Slipper 17 goes in easily.

keep a line on the boat so it doesn't drift away . . .   walk it up to the shore for rigging. (PHOTOS BY C. KING)

Various inexpensive fender-mounted trailer hitches exist. You can even find them in discount stores. Personally, if I were you, I'd hire a professional to mount a permanent hitch on my car. The bolts on the fender models can vibrate loose and you could lose the whole rig. Not only that but your runaway boat could veer into oncoming traffic and kill somebody. It's better to use an oversize hitch and then never have to worry about it again.

Boat trailers come equipped with safety chains to keep car and trailer connected should the ball and socket connection somehow break. It's a good idea to connect the chains with a padlock. Then no one will be tempted, while you're in Howard Johnson's having lunch, to unhitch

If you can really travel with your boat, the possibilities are endless.

your boat and drive away. Later, when your car and trailer are left unattended while you're out sailing, casual thieves will be discouraged from making off with your trailer.

I've always trimmed my boats to balance with just a slight weight on the tongue. They're very easy to haul around by hand that way and I've never had any problems on the road. A big empty trailer can be very tongue-heavy. Getting someone to sit on the after end will make it much easier to drag around by hand. At times, rather than go through a series of complicated back-up maneuvers, I've simply unhooked the trailer and walked it around to where I wanted it.

If you can afford it, buy a spare wheel and tire for your trailer. You can have it all blown up and ready for an emergency. Most trailer tires are small and don't take up much space. Otherwise, if your trailer gets a flat, you're stuck. Make a habit of frequently checking the tightness of your wheels and of your trailer-car connection.

If you own a boat that hauls around easily, you've got an instant camper. We've spent numerous nights on the road in our boats, pulled into the truck areas behind highway restaurants. It's cheap and you're right next to breakfast when you wake up in the morning. You can't beat that!

TO MOTOR OR NOT

At times when there's no wind (or when there's too much wind) it sure is nice to turn on some kind of motor that will get you where you're going promptly and without a lot of thrashing around. Small outboard motors are inexpensive, new or used; they adapt easily to small boats; they do the job. Why would anyone go to sea without one?

Oars

Well for one thing, it can be fun to get around without one. It's a challenge that can be entertaining. If you were in a rush, you wouldn't be sailing, now would you. If your boat is immobilized, what better time to swim, take a bath, read, make love, take a nap, organize the cabin— whatever. Calm can be nice. If the wind is excessive, you can reef down and get under a protected shore or run up on a beach if you're shoal draft. While you're waiting out the wind, what better time to swim, take a bath, read, make love, take a nap, organize the cabin, etc. Besides, outboards smell, weigh down the stern, take up space, create a fire hazard, cost money, won't start. So to hell with them. Consider the words of Philip Bolger, author, sly naval architect, skilled boat builder and innovative thinker:

"In the beginning boats were paddled and consequently had to be lowsided though they could be very long and weren't necessarily narrow. At a date not very accurately known but upwards of four thousand years ago, a genius with a blinding flash of insight made a very long paddle, set it against a fulcrum, and put the strength of his back and legs into his stroke. The next several thousand years were spent spreading the word of how well this notion worked, and refining the technique. It allowed much

Many small boats row very easily. Here the author rows his West Wight Potter.

heavier and bulkier vessels, though it had its drawbacks and never caught on among leads in ice, or up jungle creeks.

The next brainstorm was that of using the expansion of a heated gas or vapor to turn a shaft on which paddles could be mounted, whereupon the oar went out of fashion again. It never disappeared entirely, any more than the paddle had in the age of the oar, but its use declined until few people understood its potential. A time came when hardly anybody thought a boat without expanding-gas-driven paddles was useful or even prudent. Athletes worked out in strange oar-driven machines, and children played in toys maneuvered (hardly driven) with vestigial oars, but all serious movements, such as taking the dog ashore from the moored cruiser, depended on the mechanical paddles though they, too, have their drawbacks, as follows:

They're expensive, costing ten or more times as much as oars.

They're complex and temperamental, needing much care and forethought to be reliable; they don't get this care and forethought and tend to stop working at inconvenient times.

They need periodic refueling, and grow very heavy and bulky if designed to extend the intervals by carrying more fuel or by use of nuclear fission.

They're attractive to thieves in a time in which it's unusual to do anything cruel to a thief.

They're awkward and ugly objects, laborious to carry around, and they interfere with various good qualities, such as an ability to sail well.

They're messy things to come near, the best of them exuding oil and grease; many of them are also noisy enough to cover sounds which, in fog or darkness, it is well to hear."

Philip C. Bolger

Outboards

Still, look around you and everywhere you see outboards. Why? Because they are convenient. Several manufacturers make really small air-cooled models that will nudge at least a micro cruiser along nicely. An

The Elliott Power Paddle is an example of some of the very lightweight outboard motors available. 1 to 1.5 horsepower motors are quite sufficient to move a small boat around in most conditions. In very high winds, light motors cannot do the whole job but, working with a deeply reefed mainsail, they can help you make progress to windward. Take care that the wind doesn't heel the boat over so far as to pull the prop out of the water.

Evinrude 4 horsepower pushed my 22-foot MacGregor into almost any weather. The bigger the boat, the more sense auxiliary power makes. Remember, if you have a centerboard boat, handling will be much improved under power if you drop the board, at least partially, so that the boat can turn or pivot around it. With the board retracted, you may find steering sluggish or, if winds are strong, impossible. In my experience, an outboard is most useful in heavy winds, when you can simply drop your sails and motor in.

If you use an outboard, you must reserve additional space for gasoline and you'll also need space for tools, a plug wrench at least, and spare spark plugs. Still, no doubt about it, if you have a motor, there will be times you'll wonder how anyone could possibly make do without one.

Of course you can make do. For very short distances, you can paddle. Paddles are fairly compact and store easily even on small boats. Rowing is much more efficient. You can row far longer and go much farther. Even heavy sailboats can be moved surprisingly well by the ⅙-horse-

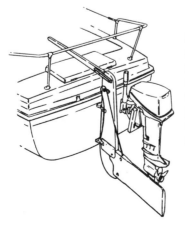

Here you see a potential problem with outboards. When the kick-up rudder is in the raised position, it can swing into contact with the outboard. Such an accident can chew up the rudder or break the shear pin on the propellor, costing you the use of your outboard, possibly at a very inopportune moment.

power produced by a man with oars. Stowing oars is more of a problem. You can lash them to the shrouds if they won't fit on deck. You also can check out various sizes of aluminum or plastic pipe and jury-rig collapsible oars that are lightweight and inexpensive.

Electric Motors

Another option is the electric trolling motor. Electrics are very lightweight. They start at the flick of a switch; they're silent; they don't smell and the battery doesn't have to take up space and add weight in the cockpit. In cost per running hours, recharging is as cheap or cheaper than gasoline. Deep-cycle rechargable batteries are not cheap, however. You'll pay at least $60, probably more. The battery will weigh much more than a full three-gallon gas tank, too, though you can store it forward somewhere. By the time you've added the cost of the battery to the cost of the motor, you could have purchased a 1.2 horsepower gas outboard. In the end, the virtues of the electric have more to do with reliability, simplicity and aesthetics (no noise, smell, etc.) than anything else. As auxiliary power for at least a micro cruiser, the electric motor deserves more attention than it's received.

For light use, an electric motor is a convenient auxiliary.

Even a 12-pound-thrust electric will move a lightweight hull.

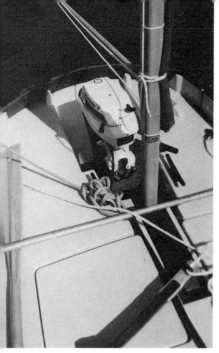

An outboard motor well makes a neat installation. This system on a Drascombe Lugger offers the virtues of an inboard motor without the complexity and expense.

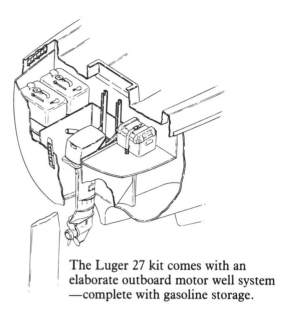

The Luger 27 kit comes with an elaborate outboard motor well system —complete with gasoline storage.

TYPICAL RUN-OUT TIMES FOR 3 ELECTRIC OUTBOARDS AT ⅔ THROTTLE

14 lb. Thrust	6 hours running time
17 lb. Thrust	5 hours running time
24 lb. (approx. 1 H.P.)	3 hours running time

What's right for you? Consider your sailing grounds. Will you be negotiating inlets or long canals? You might then need an outboard. Maybe not if your sailing mainly is on smaller lakes. Are winds fairly dependable and usually moderate? Maybe oars will be sufficient. Try going without first. Mount some oarlocks on your boat and see. Make sure the mounting is strong. Thru-bolt the oarlocks; and use a backing plate. If you can get by, you've saved yourself lots of money and freed yourself from all mechanical worries. Not only that, unpowered boats in most states require no license, no numbers, no registration fees. However, if sailing seems unsatisfactory without auxiliary power, then forget what the purists say and get a motor. You're out there for fun, after all. If not, why go?

A hidden outboard is harder to steal, neat, clean, and leaves no unsightly clutter on your stern. It looks like an inboard, but it's less expensive and much easier to repair. (PHOTO BY LUGER MANUFACTURING CO.)

*SAILING ON A
MICRO-BUDGET*

	SAIL & OARS	ELECTRIC OUTBOARD	GAS OUTBOARD
Maneuvering in harbors	Good on smaller boats	Very handy	Handy
Powering while becalmed	Good for an hour or so	Good for 4–7 hours	Good
Running inlets	Difficult, often dangerous	Only the very biggest help. Needs sail assist	Maybe the only safe and practical way
Transiting canals and rivers	Difficult, sometimes impossible, often illegal	Impractical without favorable winds	Maybe the only way
Running in high winds and seas	Oars not much help. Rely on sail. Best stay in harbor	Not much use	Very handy

SAILING WITH CHILDREN

Someone once remarked that travelling with children is like riding third class on a Bulgarian railroad. In the best of all possible worlds, the family travelling with children has the means to do it comfortably. Usually though, the couple with young children has not yet reached the peak of their earning potential. Money is tight and every choice is a compromise. It's usually after the kids are off on their own that a couple finally moves into a bigger yacht. Ironically, it's often far bigger than they need.

I propose that every young couple with kids be allowed to exchange their 20-foot boat with their parents' 34-footer. Then each family would have something more suited to its requirements. I know there are lots of good reasons why this idea won't work, still there's an irony in there somewhere. One nice thing: When you sail your little boat stuffed with coolers and children and sleeping bags into a new harbor, it *is* fun to admire the floating monuments belonging to people who've made it big and then forgot where they put it.

We digress. A book about small boat cruising needs to talk about children because it's in small boats that you'll most often find them, since small boats are all that most young families can afford. Safety becomes even more crucial when a significant portion of your crew does not understand safety consciousness, does not obey orders quickly, and does not even fully comprehend what is going on while you're under way.

Your four biggest safety concerns with children are boredom, seasickness, carelessness and, occasionally, fear.

Boredom

Sailing is an acquired taste. What is serene to an adult is boring for a child. Children need to *do* something. The best entertainment for kids is a secure spot in the bow. Behind a bow pulpit, kids can hang on, enjoy the motion and the spray, and ride happily for hours. Older children can be enlisted as jib sheet tenders or even taught to steer. When there's absolutely nothing to do but sit in the cockpit, you'll soon have problems. For this reason, it's best to break your day into a series of segments, stopping once in a while for a swim, a snack, beaching to explore an interesting cove, things like that. Kids like *being on the water* more than they like sailing—especially at first. Begin by doing things that maximize the pleasures of simply being there, gradually building the children's tolerance for longer intervals of pure sailing. Arrange to leave your kids behind with a babysitter once in a while, too. Then you can catch up on your private pleasures.

Seasickness

Seasickness is part mental, part physical. You'll notice that the people with the least to do get sick first. The bow pulpit, for all its movement, is the best guarantee against a seasick child. A few kids can play in the cabin, even in a seaway, with no ill effects. For most adults and kids, going below is a surefire way to feel worse. Motion sickness remedies, taken before you set out, are a good preventative measure. Some kids will get *very* drowsy and sleep soundly for an hour or more—sometimes longer. With my kids, sleeping off the medication doesn't seem to interfere with their normal nighttime sleep quota. It's just a natural way of dealing with discomfort. Vomiting is the other classic natural remedy for motion sickness. It often brings temporary relief. Everyone has a different tolerance for motion sickness. The best preventatives seem to be: things to do, medication, and occasional breaks in the routine to eat, swim, explore. There is no completely effective cure, nor will you likely

Going below in a seaway is a sure-fire guarantee for seasickness. In fair weather, though, the peak is an ideal child's haven, a cubbyhole to play in or to curl up and sleep.

be at sea long enough for a more lasting acclimatization to take place. One might add too, don't dwell on the issue so much as to make the condition of the children's stomach a focal point of the trip.

Carelessness

Carelessness is a natural part of childhood. It can be aggravated by boredom and mal de mer. Here's where you come in, taking care to remove any sharp or raggedy, cutting edges people might fall into, rigging a lifeline around a small child or a series of grab lines kids can use to get around on a deck from place to place, seeing to it lifejackets are worn, and so on. You can tell kids over and over again to be careful but often they don't know how yet. Cause and effect relationships that seem obvious to you are opaque to them. In a child's life more than in ours, things just seem to happen. It adds to their sense of wonder—and to their fears.

Fear

Sometimes, kids on a sailboat are going to get scared. They're afraid more than anything that the boat will be blown over. It's reassuring to tell them that the boat has flotation and therefore it can't sink. Break off a piece of foam and throw it in the water so they can *see* it floating. Act like this is a fiendishly clever thing, this flotation. Even full of water, you can tell them, the boat will float like a cake of soap.

If you're in fresh water and have a very small unsinkable boat, you can do a swamped canoe drill with your boat, removing cushions and contents from the cabin first. (If your electrical system is built in, forget it.) I did this with a small boat and let my wife and daughter swim around it for a while, climb in and out, and generally relax with it. If you can do it and have some way to get the water back out, it's an enlightening exercise.

Kids are going to be scared by and delighted by big waves. Mostly they'll be scared at first, then the next time out they'll ask you to go where the big waves are. Your attitude is crucial. If you're relaxed and enjoying yourself, your children will rapidly regain their composure. If *you're* visibly unhinged, your family will sense that and become unhinged also.

Many children, when scared, will freeze, clinging desperately to any secure handhold, even when it's best they moved. At such a time, the lap of an unoccupied adult is best. If everyone is busy, the cabin is best. Later, make a point of explaining exactly what was going on, but meanwhile, an immobilized child is likely to get hurt. Remove the child from harm's way first.

If you sail with children, assign each one a location where he or she will be out of the way when you have to do things fast—anchor, drop sails, come about. Practice having everyone go to battle stations so that it is a reflex.

Forget "port," "starboard," "bow," and "stern" for a while. Most children are slow enough doing what you tell them anyway. "Left," "right," "up there," "back here" will do fine and at least the kids will know what you're talking about. Many kids simply freeze when they're confused. Then you get mad and yell at them; then they decide you are hell to live with on a boat and won't want to go sailing with you.

Rehearse "man overboard" drills from time to time. Sometimes the skipper should pretend he's the one who fell overboard and stay completely out of the action as his family tries to rescue him. Practice storm procedures too, explaining to everyone why each thing is being done.

Boredom, seasickness, carelessness, and fear are only sometime things and should not deter you from going sailing with your kids. A discussion of safety follows. It is based on the premise that one can cruise safely and enjoyably with children if the necessary precautions have been taken ahead of time.

SAFETY

There is no particular reason why a small boat should be considered less safe at sea than a large one. After all, when great ships are abandoned, their occupants seek safety in lifeboats, which are, in fact, well-designed small boats. Rather than discuss what sorts of oceangoing accomplishments small boats are capable of (more on that in Part III), let's discuss instead those things a safety-conscious mariner should have in mind when setting out in a small sailing cruiser.

Boat Flotation

Virtually all small sailing boats now manufactured in the U.S. are equipped with flotation of one sort or another—usually foam blocks. Isn't it nice to know, whatever else might happen to you, you can't sink? If the boat draws less than a foot or two and has flotation, then even in a hard fix (I'd call being capsized a hard fix) you can simply stay with your boat until it blows ashore or someone picks you up. The key is to *stay with your boat*, not exhaust yourself trying to swim to a shore that might be out of reach. Better your boat should eventually wash up on the beach than your remains. I can't be more blunt than that. *Don't remove flotation to gain additional stowage space.* How will you find words to apologize to your family while you're all treading water out in the middle of nowhere.

After all, the great virtue of these little boats is the absence of worry they offer. Keep your boat floating; keep it upright. You certainly should have a pump to remove water from the cabin. Hand pumps are quite inexpensive. Better, but more expensive, are pumps *mounted in the cockpit* that remove water from inside the boat. A bucket in the hands of a frightened sailor is a very effective water-removal system. Big sponges are best for getting out the small stuff.

Even swamped, some boats are capable of making headway. If your outboard weighs down the stern, unbolt it and let it sink. It's only a thing. Don't worry about it. Stay afloat. Stay upright. Even if the wind is going to pile you up on the rocks ashore, don't worry about it. It's not your life savings and the boat—probably—is insured. Once you hit shore, you can walk out on dry land and you and your family will be safe. First things first.

You can do lots of things to add flotation. Empty plastic milk cartons add flotation and you can stuff them into odd places. Cheap inflatable swim toys can be used, too. See if inflatable mattresses can be used in place of foam ones. Figure roughly that a cubic yard of flotation will support a thousand pounds of boat and equipment.

In a Storm

Reduce sail when the wind picks up. It's less strain on the boat, less anxiety for the children, and the boat will be in better control. And, it's more comfortable. Courage and manhood have nothing to do with it. Only a fool sails over-canvassed in a blow. Often just dropping the jib will be sufficient. If you do that, pull your centerboard part of the way up to re-balance the boat. Better yet, reef the main and leave the jib up. The boat will handle better and, should the wind increase yet again, you can then drop the jib.

If you're anticipating a squall, run your boat up on a sandy beach until it passes. (Here's one reason why I'm partial to beachable designs in small sailing cruisers.) If you're far from shelter and have to ride it out, consider the following.

1. Get your kids comfortable in the cabin. Tell them they're in for some *real* excitement. If you tell them not to be afraid, they'll start immediately to get afraid—just like they do when you tell them something isn't going to hurt. Make them put on their life jackets.
2. Get the sails down. You may be able to use the jib, but for a real live squall, it's best to have everything down and made fast.
3. You can ensure staying upright by lowering your centerboard (if you have one). You'll need your centerboard down anyway to improve your directional control under power. Tie a life jacket around the mast and run it up as high on the mast as it'll go. If you are knocked down,

As the wind kicks up, this Montego 20 has its sails furled and bagged and is motoring in to safety.

(almost impossible with the sails down) the life jacket will see to it that the mast cannot be rolled under. Be sure to rig a downhall on the life jacket to get it down again when the blow is over.

4. If you have an outboard, make sure its tank is full (if it has an integral tank) and get it started. You can use it to keep your nose into the waves and to maintain steerageway. Don't pound into the waves; keep just enough throttle for directional control. Easy does it. If you only have oarpower, you can use them for the same purpose, but don't exhaust yourself. Just keep your bow into the wind.

5. Another way to keep your nose into the wind is to let out your anchor and most of its line. It will act as a drogue to slow you down as you back away, nose to the seas. Pull your rudder out so as not to strain it, or tie it off amidships. In shallow water, the anchor will take a bite and keep you from grounding. If you *want* to ground, either pull the anchor up or, if you must, let the line go with a float on the end (a milk jug or life jacket) so you can retrieve it later. Drogues or sea anchors are available, too. These are small canvas cones that create a lot of drag when trailed on a line. If you *don't* want to be blown to shore, these are a good investment. They stow flat and take up little space.

6. If you must, run under bare pole before the wind. Don't motor downwind at high speed; you might broach. Easy does it.

7. To sum, whatever you may have read in various accounts of ocean voyagers caught in storms at sea, I would suggest you play it safe. You're probably *not* going to be on the high seas anyway. Concentrate on keeping your boat upright and afloat, letting its natural buoyancy do the rest. Seek shelter if you can. If you can't, get the sails down, make the boat watertight, start your outboard if you have one, and ride it out. Once you realize how safe you are, you might even enjoy the excitement.

Keeping Yourself Afloat

The coast guard requires everyone on board your vessel to have a "personal flotation device." Most people refuse to wear them. I confess, I only put one on in rough weather. Many children put up a continual fuss when made to wear them, which is a shame since they often *must* do so—fuss or not. It's worthwhile to take the kids to the chandlery to try on and pick the life jacket they like—even if their choice is the most expensive model. The cheap orange ones are often lumpy and uncomfortable.

Protect your children. Get them comfortable life jackets they'll wear without complaint.

It's reasonable to have a policy for each of the three "zones" on board: cabin, cockpit, foredeck and cabin top. In the cabin, I don't think kids need jackets. Non-swimmers do need them the moment they emerge. Swimmers, in the cockpit, can sit on "throwable" life cushions, but need life jackets when they leave the cockpit. In lousy weather, wear jackets in the cockpit as well as forward.

For nighttime sailing, some form of waterproof light and a plastic police whistle should be pinned to each life jacket and kids should wear the jackets whenever they're out of the cabin. In any kind of "weather," so should the adults.

If you're an adult and you can't stand life jackets, an inflatable pillow, folded flat and stuffed into a back pocket, would be a nice margin of safety should you fall overboard. You could quickly blow it up and stuff it under your shirt. Buoyant windbreaker jackets are on the market now, too. Flotation need not be uncomfortable and is always a vital margin of safety.

Safety harnesses are a good investment and pad-eyes properly reinforced can be added when needed. Watch your kids move about the boat and figure out where they should be able to clip themselves on. At night, harnesses are a must as well as the small, waterproof lights that clip on to life vests.

To Avoid Falling Overboard—

1. Stay seated most of the time.
2. Have lots of firm handholds. Be able to go from handhold to handhold, bow to cockpit. Teach your children (and your guests) how to move safely on a boat, in a wrestler's crouch always holding onto something, not striding around like someone walking across a living room.
3. A bow pulpit is a worthwhile investment, especially for kids, who love being up there.
4. Lifelines on raised stanchions can trip you up on a very small boat. Deck construction on many small boats is such that stanchions might tear out should a full-grown man fall into one with real force. Better security is to add some extra grab rails to the cabin top. Lifelines from a stern pulpit to the aft cabin wall, enclosing the cockpit, are a fine idea —especially if you have children aboard.
5. Trunk cabins are better than flush decks on small boats. Flush decks, when wet and the boat is heeled over, become slick sliding boards. You can sit on a cabin top and inch your way along.
6. Get white bathing suits for young children. My father-in-law insisted that all his children wear white bathing suits while they learned to swim. White suits are much easier to spot underwater. During family summers on Buzzards Bay, the kids lived in the water. Because of the highly visible suits, he claims, two drownings were averted.
7. Pay attention to what's going on. This is a habit that takes time to cultivate. It's good training for kids.

Getting Back on Board

Now you've gone and done it. You've fallen overboard. Or maybe you went for a swim but didn't plan in advance how to get back aboard. You swim up, drape your arm over the gunwale and . . . and what? You're treading water; nothing to push off of there. Clearly this is going to be a gymnastic challenge. How strong are you? Can *all* members of the family

The cockpit of this Sirius 20 is well protected with a stern pulpit and lifelines. Note the boarding ladder on the transom.

muscle themselves back up? Can your kids even reach the gunwale? Planning is required before anyone goes over the side, whether by hook or by crook. What to do?

The best solution is to mount a folding ladder on the transom. Now *everybody* can get on board. Be sure to back up any through-hull fittings with oversize washers or, better yet, large plywood pads backed by washers. (While you're at it, back up all your cleats, too. Manufacturers often scrimp here.)

If a ladder is too costly, a loop of line hooked over a cleat on the cockpit coaming can give you something to hook your foot into for a leg-up into the boat. Make sure the cleat and the fiberglass there are properly supported to take that kind of strain. If need be, add a well-reinforced fitting that will hold a boarding loop. Passing the line through a six-inch length of heavy garden hose will provide a more comfortable purchase for your foot. In most small boats, the loop is sufficient. A rope ladder is good, though it takes up more room.

Investigate mounting a step on your rudder—on the side *opposite* your outboard mount. You might mount a rope loop from the bottom gudgeon of your rudder for an emergency foothold.

As in most things, answers are not hard to come by if you ask the question in time.

This might be a good point to discuss swimming children. You'll get a lot of peace of mind if your kids wear some form of flotation—if only a single "water muscle" while they're swimming. You might ask them to swim off the stern—where you can see them. Children tend to be lost from view as they swim around to the bow.

If you're riding at anchor, you'll notice that most small boats tend to "sail" around a lot, wander back and forth on their line. A very young and weak swimmer could be pushed under the boat as it started its gradual swing in the opposite direction. This risk should be explained clearly to little children and they should be confined to where you can see them. They can hold on to lines with fat knots at the end or loops. You can festoon the boat with such lines if your children are very young. Mooring lines are perfect. Dangle one from the bow, one from each of the stays, and one from each of the stern cleats. Before the children go in, you should check the water, first. Currents, even small ones, can be tough to see and even tougher to swim against, especially for small children. In any current a life jacket and line are necessary. Most kids love the water. They'll probably much prefer swimming to sailing. It pays to establish safety procedures right away.

"Man Overboard"

Practice throwing a life jacket over the side and sailing back to get it. Try that on all points of sail. Direct someone to do nothing but keep the "swimmer" in view at all times. Life jackets should have plastic police whistles pinned to them and, at night, small clip-on flashlights.

The moment someone goes over the side, throw over a flotation cushion right away. If a child goes over, an adult should go over, too, to lend aid and encouragement.

The person who bought the boat should *not* be the only person who knows how to sail it. See to that.

When all's said and done, it's faster to start the outboard, let the sails flap (or drop them) and *carefully* motor back to pick the swimmer up.

Fire On Board

Many small boats don't have forward hatches. The only way into (and out of) the cabin is through the main hatch. Don't cook with your stove blocking the way out. A fire could trap someone in the cabin. It's best to cook outside in the cockpit away from the outboard motor and its gas tank. A marine hibachi can be clipped onto a bow or stern pulpit and will keep the cooking completely outboard. In rainy weather, if you're confined to the cabin, you may need to warm something up. Be mindful not to block your exit. Have a place to safely set down hot pans, which will burn or melt fabric and badly scar fiberglass. A plywood strip stored under a bed cushion is ideal. Make it big enough to support both stove and two pans. Things are less apt to be overturned that way and you can move the whole operation topside when the weather clears.

Mount a fire extinguisher on a bulkhead where you can get at it quickly, even from the cockpit.

Conclusion

Don't let this chapter scare you or dissuade you from sailing. The difference between an adventure and a crisis is that the former challenge was anticipated and prepared for and the latter case was not. With children aboard, it is even more crucial to remain composed and deliberate in your actions. Radiate confidence born out of good planning and careful preparation.

BOAT BASICS

PART III

THE HULL

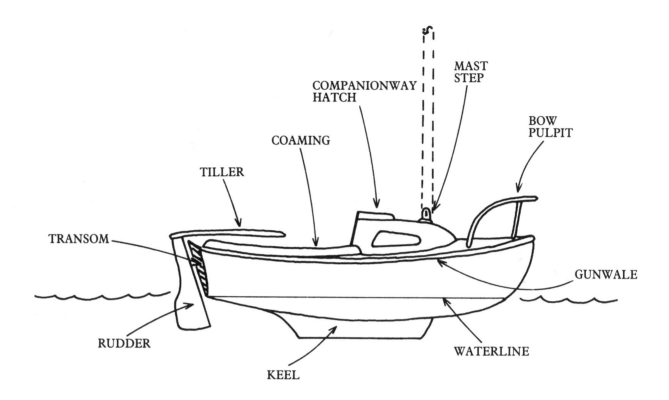

COMPANIONWAY HATCH

MAST STEP

BOW PULPIT

COAMING

TILLER

TRANSOM

GUNWALE

RUDDER

WATERLINE

KEEL

SOME NAUTICAL TERMS

Draft
The maximum depth of a boat from the waterline to the bottom of the keel or centerboard.

Freeboard
The height of the hull from the gunwale to the waterline.

Beam
The maximum width of a boat.

L.O.A.
Length over all. The boat's maximum length.

L.O.D.
Length on deck, not counting bowsprits for example.

L.W.L.
Length on the waterline. This measurement says a lot about how fast a boat will be.

Displacement
What a boat weighs.

Ballast
Weight added, usually in the keel, to help a boat stay upright.

Gunwale
The upper edge of the hull . . . where the hull and deck meet.

Transom
The flat after end of a boat. Canoe shaped hulls have no transom.

Coaming
A raised edge around the cockpit that keeps water out and serves also as a backrest. High coamings mean comfort.

Pulpit
An elevated railing, usually in the bow.

Bilge
The area under the floor of the cabin. Loose water tends to collect in there and turn foul, hence the old sailor's derisive term "bilgewater!"

In the simplest terms, the hull is what keeps the water out and what keeps you in. Its shape, especially its shape below the waterline, has a profound effect on the performance and liveability of your vessel.

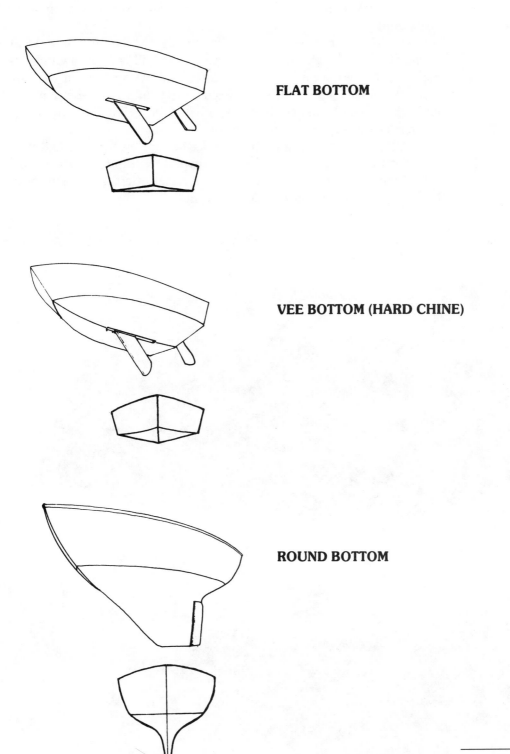

FLAT BOTTOM

VEE BOTTOM (HARD CHINE)

ROUND BOTTOM

Let's start with the simplest hull shape and consider its strengths and virtues. The flat-bottom hull—like a rowboat hull—is about as simple as you can get. A narrow flat-bottom hull can be quite fast under sail; a wider hull will be slower but will have enormous stability. The flat-bottom boat will draw only a few inches, making it ideal for fishing or just snooping around over tidal flats and other shallow places where most boats can't go.

In choppy water, especially at higher speeds, the flat-bottom hull will pound the fillings right out of your teeth. The hull takes an awful beating, too. Without a lot of power, a broad hull will be beaten back by each wave it encounters. It's not a blue-water hull. A flat-bottom hull under sail would be blown sideways; it has so little "bite" on the water. A centerboard is the most common solution for that.

Finally, if you mount a cabin on a flat-bottom boat, you'll find very little headroom in there. Still there are appealing features to the simple flat-bottom boat and a number of commercial offerings, mostly open boats, feature flat-bottom, shallow-draft hulls.

Here's the great appeal of the extremely shallow draft boat. This Marsh Hen is sitting happily in ankle-deep water making it, and boats like it, ideal for exploring and shoreside camping. (PHOTO BY FLORIDA BAY BOAT CO.)

There's a fairly simple solution to reduce the pounding and improve the rough-water performance of the flat-bottom hull without losing much of that wonderful stability. It's called a vee-bottom. This shape is still very simple to fabricate and it's used in thousands of lightweight aluminum skiffs as well as in many do-it-yourself plywood designs. The vee is fairly sharp in the bow, helping the boat part the waves as it moves into a chop. Then the vee flattens out aft offering a nearly flat bottom in the stern, where the cockpit is, where people are most apt to sit and move around. This type of hull is also called a "hard chined" hull, referring to the hard edge partway up the hull where the sides and the vee-bottom meet.

Vee-bottom boats can be very seaworthy. They have very good stability and tend to heel very little, preferring to sail on their bottoms. In a small boat, the vee is probably the best shape.

Round Hulls

The final option is the round hull. It's deeper, can't plane or surf down waves the way the flat- or vee-bottom can, nor is it apt to find its way into very shallow water without running aground. On the other hand, the deep hull offers a very comfortable ride in heavy seas and has lots of headroom and storage below. With its ballast weight down deep, the round hull will heel easily at first, then become progressively stiffer. Whereas a flat-bottom boat can, if somehow flipped, be stable upside down, the deep keel boat cannot. It has "ultimate" stability. That makes it the top choice for deep-water sailers.

Few small boats offer the full keel. Cape Cod Shipbuilding offers an 18-footer called the Goldeneye. It's been sailed across the Atlantic. Cape Dory builds the 19-foot Typhoon. Both boats have bunks for four inside. To my mind, I prefer beachability and portability in a small boat, but both of these full-keelers evolved in Buzzard's Bay (where there's

For sea-going craft, the deep hull offers the best ride, best ultimate stability, and greatest volume for storage. This boat, the 20-foot Flicka, can carry well over a ton of supplies for extended cruising.

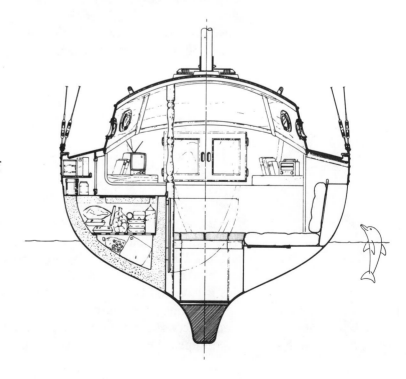

The Cape Dory Typhoon offers a full keel in a 19-foot hull.

often a nasty chop) and most of their owners moor the boats out all season and sail them everywhere much larger yachts go. For these applications, they're perfect.

Any boat that's going to sail to windward has to have some system to keep it from being pushed sideways by the wind and waves. The full-keel boat has no such problem; shallow-draft boats, however, have to come up with something. Let's look at the various possible approaches to solving the slippage problem.

UNDER THE WATERLINE
Leeboards

The Dutch solved the problem, after the Renaissance, by adding "leeboards" to their shallow-draft vessels. These could be lowered underwater while tacking to provide some lateral resistance. The "shallop," a small open boat with leeboards and a spritsail, carried on the *Mayflower* was used by the Pilgrims to explore the New England coast. The system is still in use in a few modern vessels. Leeboards have several virtues. They are inexpensive and simple to install. They leave the interior of the boat free of trunks, pulleys and winches. On a small boat, this is a special blessing. The bottom of the hull is smooth and flat for easy beaching. On the negative side, most people think leeboards look strange, consequently only a courageous manufacturer will build boats so equipped. Leeboards are usually light and thus offer no ballast advantage when lowered. Still, for very small boats, leeboards are underutilized considering all their advantages.

Centerboards

The centerboard gained great popularity in colonial times and has remained popular ever since. Housed in a trunk along the boat's centerline, the board swivels up and out of the way when beaching or when not in use. The board can be weighted to add to stability. The so-called "swing keel" is simply a very heavy wing-like centerboard that contributes enormous stability at the expense of imposing corresponding strains on the centerboard trunk. Centerboards require some system of pulleys or winches to get them up and down. They also intrude on the cabin space, dividing the cabin in half on smaller boats. Accommodations on larger boats can be designed around the trunk. Smaller boats simply are stuck with it. In very small boats, the central location of the centerboard trunk makes it hard to find a good location for the marine toilet—a further inconvenience. Although a centerboard boat beaches easily, one also must be careful that the trunk doesn't get packed with sand and shells, for then you'll shove off and find you can't get your board down. It's advisable to carry a small saw aboard to slip between the board and the trunk to get the sand out.

A beachable boat like this Spindrift is ideal for exploring and camping.

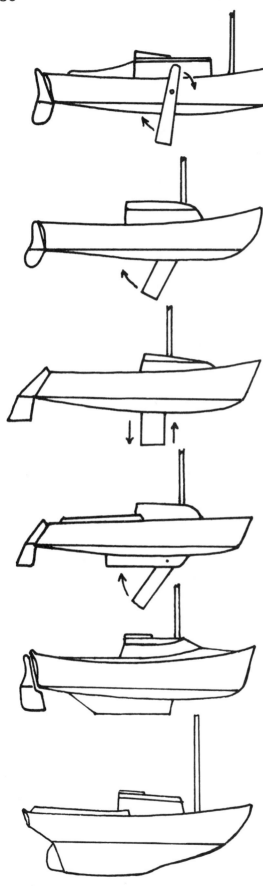

LEEBOARDS

Unconventional, may be vulnerable to damage. Simple. Inexpensive. Does not intrude into cabin. Beachable.

CENTERBOARD (SWING KEEL)

Widely used. Also offers shallow draft. Weighted, can offer stability. Intrudes into cabin space.

DAGGER OR DROP KEEL

Will not kick up if grounded. Less drag underway—faster. Simpler in a small boat. Can add stability. Intrusive.

KEEL/CENTERBOARD

Keel adds stability; board is light and is easily handled. Reasonably shallow draft. No intrusions into cabin.

SHALLOW (SKEG) KEEL

Simple. No intrusions into cabin space. Cannot be beached easily. (Twin keels can). Harder to ramp launch.

FULL KEEL

Still preferred for ocean cruising. Deep hull—good for storage. Impossible to beach; very hard to ramp launch.

All told, despite its occasional inconveniences, centerboard variations dominate the small-boat market because they're familiar and because they usually perform well.

Daggerboards

Whereas the centerboard swivels up and down around a pin, the daggerboard simply drops straight down into its trunk sheath. The daggerboard trunk takes up less space and, if it's light in weight, the board can simply be raised and lowered by hand. On heavy boards, a winch is needed. Several modern designs use the daggerboard as a "drop keel." The boat can be launched from a trailer, then the heavy keel is lowered in place and left there until it's time to take the boat out again. Now it's a keel boat; now it isn't.

There are drawbacks to the daggerboard concept in heavier boats. If the boat strikes something on the bottom at speed, the board can't kick up out of the way as a centerboard can. All the impact will be absorbed by the centerboard trunk. Neither can a sailor modify the underwater shape of his boat by partially raising the board to move the center of resistance aft, as he can with a centerboard. Despite these objections, a number of very high performance boats have been introduced with daggerboards and they're selling well.

Keels

The Vikings seem to have been the first shipwrights to have put any kind of fin keel under their boats. Their vessels had shallow, full-length keels. Coupled with their advanced sailing techniques, Viking ships could make progress to windward. Several modern designs, notably the English series of Drascombe boats, still use variants of this ancient system.

Keels offer a strong backbone for the boat and great simplicity. No winches, no kick-up rudders, and no trunk poking up into the cabin interior. Keels don't permit you to actually beach your boat nor do they kick up when you run aground. When you're stuck, you're stuck, though usually not for long.

SHOAL KEELS

Many small boats these days feature shallow "skeg" keels. With airfoil shapes, these keels provide effective if not astounding windward ability and reasonably shallow draft—often as little as two feet. Such designs offer many of the virtues of both centerboard and keel designs and are gaining market acceptance.

FULL KEELS

For ultimate performance against the wind, a deep keel is best. Twelve Meter sloops have deep keels; most ocean voyagers do, too. You get good ultimate stability with that weight down there and can carry more sail because of it. For even small boats, though, beaching is out of the question. For getting ashore you might even need a dinghy, which would be silly in a small boat. On the other hand, maybe you can moor your boat somewhere and will be in deep water most of the time. Then you'll appreciate the full keel boat's ability to bash to windward.

This deep keeled Goldeneye 18 by Cape Cod Shipbuilding has been successfully sailed across the Atlantic. Small can still be seaworthy.

Twin Keels

Several British designs solve the falling tide problem by putting two keels under their boats so they can take to the bottom easily. They gain this advantage by paying a performance penalty in increased drag.

Bilge Keels

Another solution to the grounding problem is to start with a very shallow long keel and add two small additional fins where the twin keels might have been placed on a different vessel. The area of all three fins adds up to the area of one big one and you've got a shallow boat that sits level on the beach. Windward performance is acceptable but not exceptional. This approach is a very appealing one for small sailboats, the deep cabin of a keel boat, the very shallow draft of a centerboarder . . . almost perfect!

Keel/Centerboard Designs

A final compromise is to house a thin centerboard inside a shoal keel. This provides for shallow draft, good windward performance, and no intrusions into the cabin interior. The system is relatively expensive to manufacture and won't beach perfectly level but it's the most recent approach to obtaining the best of both worlds.

Summary

Perhaps even more than sail shape, hull shape will determine what kind of sailing you're going to do and what the interior of your boat is going to look like. Personally, I like extremely shallow draft in a small boat. Any beach can be a port in a storm. And I expect to trailer my boat a lot and haul it in and out of the water frequently. We also like to pull up on a deserted beach to explore, picnic or camp overnight. This seems to be small boating at its best. But our applications are not everyone's. Other designs offer other virtues.

Most importantly, try to anticipate what kind of sailing you want to do and select the best hull design for that purpose. Fortunately, there is an enormous range of choices available in every size boat you might want. Small boats are so inexpensive you might consider buying two different ones so you don't have to compromise if you want a boat to sail to Catalina but your spouse's passion is looking for shells!

SAILING RIGS

Many excellent texts are available on how to sail, which is a subject beyond the scope of this book. Some of the best or newest of these titles are listed in the appendix. What is of major concern in this book are the different kinds of sailing rigs in use today and the advantages and disadvantages they pose to the small-boat sailor.

There are several vantage points from which we can examine any sail plan: cost, performance, ease of handling, and the ease with which we can add sail in light wind or reduce it in heavy weather. Any rig is a compromise; only you can decide which factors are most critical in the kind of sailing you propose to do.

TACKING

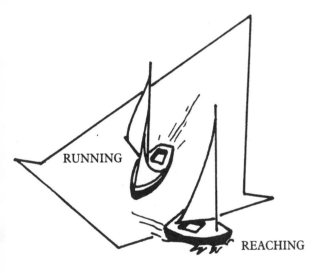

RUNNING

REACHING

SOME SAILING TERMS

Getting "in irons" or "in stays" . . .

sometimes while tacking, a boat rounds up into the wind too slowly and comes to a standstill, nose to the wind, sails flapping mightily. A boat is usually quite happy to stay in this position, so getting out of "stays" sometimes takes some effort.

Gybing . . .

gybing is zigging and zagging while running *down wind.* Instead of "coming about" *into* the wind, the wind suddenly catches on the opposite side of the sail and hurls it across the cockpit—often with great force. This move must be done with great care. Accidental gybes can capsize a small boat, damage rigging, or even hurt someone.

"Broaching to"

is a problem that occasionally pops up while running down wind in very rough seas. A large wave can push the stern around, throwing the boat sideways and possibly causing a capsize. Broaching and, *"being pooped,"* having a wave break over the stern, are signals that it's time to *"heave to,"* ride it out with reduced sails up or *"lie ahull,"* ride it out with sails down.

"Reefing" . . .

the prudent act of reducing sail when the wind gets up —by tying off a panel of sail or by rolling part of it around the boom or the mast.

Tacking . . .

tacking, pointing, beating, are all terms for zigging and zagging *up wind.* Most boats can point within 45° of the wind; some do better.

Reaching

Reaching is sailing at angles up to 90° *across the wind.* Most boats are fastest doing this.

Running down wind

is drier and more comfortable but often entails great strains on the rig and requires great concentration at the tiller.

A traditional boom and gaff catboat

SAILING RIGS

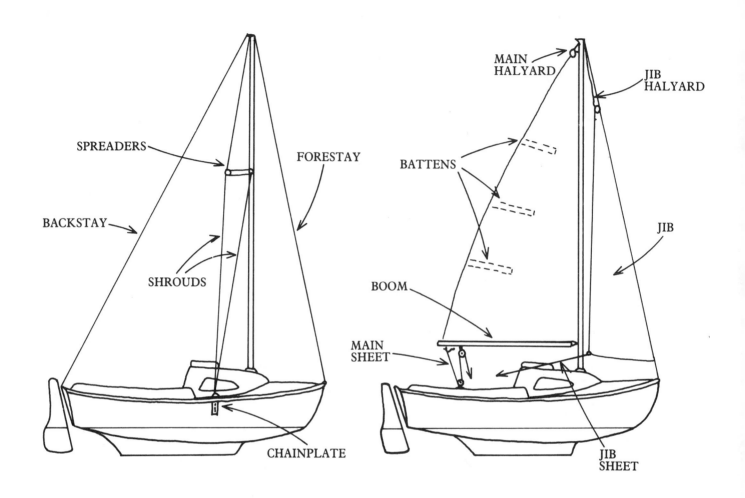

Stays or shrouds

Fixed lines, usually wire, that keep the mast standing and distribute the strains of sail pressure to the hull.

Halyards

Lines used to raise and lower the sails.

Sheets

Lines used to pull in and let out the mainsail and jib.

Battens

Fiberglass or wooden strips used to stiffen sails and reduce flapping.

Mast

Poles used to hold the sails up.

Booms

Horizontal poles used to extend sails out away from the mast.

Sprits

Poles, often hung diagonally from the mast, that can be tensioned with a block and tackle, to adjust the shape of the sail.

If I could design my own getaway small cruiser—especially if it was light and under 17 feet long—it would have one unstayed aluminum mast, which just plugged into the deck at the bow, and only one sail. The sail would be a modern triangular design. Such a rig would be light, inexpensive, efficient to windward, and easy to set up and take down.

Single-sailed rigs, called catboats, have been around for a long time of course. The traditional catboats were working craft—heavy, broad beamed, massively built, with shallow centerboards and boom and gaff sails. Modern sloops point higher and go faster, but then, as Garry Hoyt has recently shown with his "Freedom" designs, so will a modern catboat.

There's a possible drawback that could affect some small cat rigged boats. On most catboats either the mast or a mast support is going to come through the cabin—usually through the foot of the vee berth. This intrusion might block off precious foot room on berths usually cramped anyway and it might divide the bunk in half, making overnighting a somewhat less romantic experience.

Various objections notwithstanding, the cat rig offers good sailing and enormous advantages in cost, simplicity, and ease of set up and stowage. I'd love to see some manufacturers offer an unstayed cat rig as an option.

The Sloop Rig

Most sailboats, even small ones, are sloop rigged, which is to say that the mast is mounted further aft than it is on a catboat, and that a second sail or jib is hung from the forestay. On such a rig, the supporting network of stays can become complex. Most 22-foot boats will usually have a forestay, a backstay and two stays (or shrouds) per side (an upper and a lower). Smaller boats can get away with as few as three stays. New boats are usually given a sloop rig for market appeal alone. It does have its virtues.

Reducing sail on a sloop is a fairly straightforward procedure. Many small boats sail acceptably well on their mainsail alone and so, in heavy wind, one can simply drop the jib.

A reefed main and jib make a more balanced rig. Some small boats can take down both sails and sail on their genoa, if they have one, at this point. Larger boats often have storm jibs to fly with reefed mains—or they have reef points on their jibs. In such wind conditions you had best be in harbor. Reefed main and no jib will give you some control in most boats. At some point, you will have taken in so much sail that the pressure of the wind on the hull, cabin, and rigging will begin to overpower what little sail you have left and you will no longer be able to make any progress against the wind. Small boats will generally reach this point sooner than large ones. At that point, it wouldn't matter what kind of rig you're using. Short of this extremity, the sloop has a lot of flexibility, gives you lots of options.

The sloop has a few drawbacks, however. It is more complex than an unstayed modern cat rig; there are more lines to foul up; more can go wrong. Two lines are required to control the jib, one on each side of the boat. One of the crew must watch for that every time you come about.

The Freedom 21, a modern fully battened cat rig enjoying a 40-knot breeze.

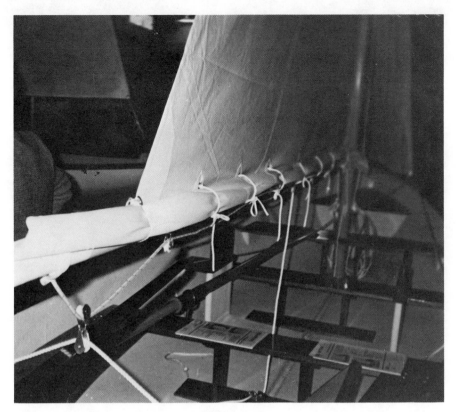

Tying in a reef reduces sail area in high winds.

The jib sheets should be folded in half, then threaded through the clew of the jib.

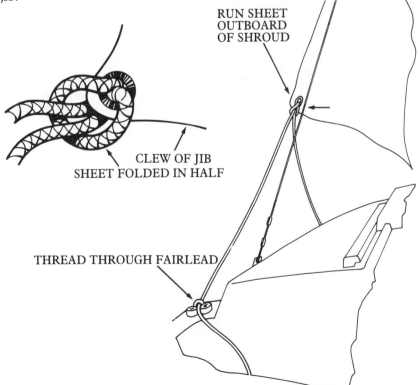

RUN SHEET
OUTBOARD
OF SHROUD

CLEW OF JIB
SHEET FOLDED IN HALF

THREAD THROUGH FAIRLEAD

Boat Basics

Imagine a standard sloop rigged sailboat. Add a second jib out there (a "flying jib," as it's called) and you have a cutter. The cutter has some virtues. The staysail plus the regular jib have about the same effect as a genoa. In moderate air, you take down one of the jibs (or roller furl it); in light air you put it up. On traditional cutters, the mast is stepped further aft, offering more balanced sail combinations. Many circumnavigators prefer cutter rigs for this reason.

In really small boats, despite the salty appearance, I think the cutter adds more complexity than it's worth. You have more stays, more sheets, more halyards, three sails to keep trimmed and drawing.

More Than One Mast?

With the exception of the "cat ketch" rig (two unstayed masts, one self-tending sail apiece) what has been said of the cutter rig applies here as well. If the object is to make a miniature of some favorite old timer, well and good. If the object is simplicity of installation and operation coupled with low cost and reliability, you want to eliminate every stick, every wire, every line and every cleat you can. Keep it simple.

SAIL SHAPES
The Square Sails

By far the oldest and most used sail shape, historically, is the square sail. For running down wind, it's still the best. Perhaps the Vikings were the world's best square sail sailors. By using what they called a beitass pole to hold the windward clew out against the wind, the vikings actually could tack. Our term "beating" to windward comes from that pole they used.

VIKING SQUARE RIGGER

TRADITIONAL SPRIT
Very handy
Not too efficient
Fairly easily reefed
Often unstayed

LUG RIG
Handy
Fairly efficient
Fairly easily reefed
Unstayed or simple stays

BOOM AND GAFF
Awkward at times
Fairly efficient
Can be awkward to reef
Simple stays

The Greeks or the Romans were the first to modify the square sail for better windward work. They moved the mast into the bow and hung the sail behind it like a flag and supported the loose upper corner by running out a diagonal pole called a "sprit." By pulling the sprit up against the mast, the sail could be collapsed easily and spiral-wrapped around the mast when not in use. This concept is so simple and handy that traditional watercraft use it still.

Although the sprit is less weatherly than a modern sail, it *will* sail into the wind fairly well. It has no boom to crack anyone on the head (although a flapping sheet block will) and its simple furling is easy to love. The sprit can be reefed by lowering it on the mast and tying a reef around the soft foot.

THE LUG SAIL

An even simpler development of the square sail was the lug rig. Imagine a square sail cocked at an angle with one loose clew tied tight to the base of the mast and the other one left free to be handled with a sheet like a fore and aft sail. One can easily imagine this as an on-the-spot improvisation by some ancient mariner. A tomb painting in ancient Haifa, in Israel, shows such a rig. Like the sprit, the lug has persisted into modern times. The sail shape is no longer square but cut with a higher peak. The Chinese developed a fully battened lug sail in classical times which we call the "junk" rig. This variant reefs so easily that many modern yachtsmen have adapted it for their use. The concept of full-length battens to "domesticate" a sail has been applied to modern sails, too, with great success—especially with tall catamaran rigs.

THE BOOM AND GAFF

This was the last variant of the square sail before the triangular sail came into use. Not only is the rig aesthetically pleasing but it offers the virtues of a short mast, a simple system of stays and a simple emergency reefing option. By simply letting the peak of the gaff down, one can "scandalize" the sail to one half its working area. This was an old sailors' trick when caught in a sudden squall—and it still works. The boom and gaff can, of course, be reefed properly by lowering the sail and tying a panel off around the boom. With its low profile, the boom and gaff lends great stability to the boats that use it and for that reason it is still preferred by many.

There are disadvantages to the rig too. The boom and gaff, even with the peak pulled up tight, cannot outpoint a modern sail, all things being equal. There is more complexity aloft and more weight and hardware where you least want it—high above the deck.

Triangular Sails

THE LATEEN SAIL

Ancient Egyptian art shows a variant of the square sail in use on the Nile. There is the usual yard at the mast head to hang the sail but the sail shape is triangular with its bottom corner tied to the base of the mast. I'm guessing that this rig was adapted, as was the lug, by some enterprising seaman who untied the clew from the base of the mast and led it aft, causing the yard to swivel down in the familiar manner of the Arabian dhows. Such a sail would vastly improve windward work, although even the modern Arabs, who still use the rig, say that "only a fool or a Christian sails to windward."

The "modern" lateen is most commonly used on very small daysailers. Although little can be done to control its sail shape, the lateen has a very low profile which lends great stability to the boats that use it. A small sailing cruiser could be easily converted to use a single lateen sail. The lateen rig does sweep the deck area ahead of the mast, however. This could make anchoring and other forward work awkward.

THE BERMUDA SAIL

The purely triangular sail or "Bermuda" sail is a relatively modern innovation made possible by improvements in rigging and mast construction. In earlier times, the tall "Bermuda rig" mast wouldn't have held together for long. There are a variety of "go fast" adaptations to control sail shape and thus improve speed. Triangular sails are easily reefed with reef points or by rolling part of the sail around the boom.

WISHBONES

Some of the earliest triangular sails used in this country didn't have booms at all but used "sprits." Whereas a sail full of air will lift the boom, causing a pocket to form and spoiling sail shape, with a sprit, the lower edge of the sail holds the tip of the sprit down (like a vang) and sail shape can be controlled simply by adjusting the tension of the sprit. The simple elegance of this concept is spoiled only by the disturbance in the sail shape caused by the sprit itself when, on one of the two windward tacks, the wind presses the sail flat against the sprit. The "wishbone" solves that problem by being curved, thus not spoiling the sail's shape. On little boats though, the straight sprit can be laid against the mast and wrapped up with the sail. This is a clean and neat system of furling.

Reefing sprit rigs is trickier. Most small boats reef by rolling part of the sail around the mast. Some gather a slab of sail against the mast with lines called "brails." Such a system is simple and fast.

SUMMARY

The most common small boat rig is the sloop with modern triangular sails. It does most things best. For a small catboat, I think I'd try a triangular wishbone rig. For ultra simple knocking about I'd prefer a traditional sprit or maybe a lateen—especially if my boat was tender and I wanted my center of effort as close to the water as I could get it. One nice thing about a really small boat, you can almost afford to experiment—try things out—see what works best. You might like two different rigs for different conditions and could take your pick. Bear in mind before you destroy anything on a stock boat that the hull and rig were designed to go together. I would have a good solid reason before I made a change.

DEVELOPMENTS OF THE ARABIC LATEEN SAIL

LATEEN RIG
Very simple
Good for "tippy" boats
Fairly efficient
Can be awkward to reef
Usually unstayed

MODERN TRIANGULAR SAIL
Simple
Most efficient
Easy to reef
Usually stayed, sometimes stays are complex

WISHBONE RIG
Fairly simple
Efficient
Reefing easy but system can be complex
Usually unstayed

SMALL BOAT RIGS

CATBOAT
Cheapest
Simplest
Reasonably efficient
Easy to handle
Preferred for boats 17 feet and under, new concepts work on even bigger boats

SLOOP
Reasonable cost
Reasonably simple
More versatile
Most efficient
Fairly easy to handle
Preferred by most designers, a close second choice

CUTTER
More costly
Complex
Versatile
Reasonably efficient
Complex to handle
Better suited for larger ocean cruising vessels

CAT KETCH
More costly
Reasonably simple
Fairly versatile
Reasonably efficient
Fairly easy to handle
A good rig for 20 footers and up.

KETCH AND YAWL
Most costly
Most complex
Very versatile
Less efficient
Complex to handle
Better suited for larger ocean cruising vessels.

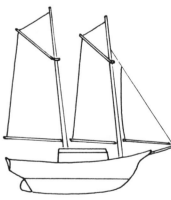

SCHOONER
Most costly
Most complex
Fairly versatile
Least efficient
Complex to handle
More a nostalgic choice than a practical one for a small boat.

A BRIEF HISTORY

Boating for pleasure is hardly a new idea. Cleopatra enjoyed occasional excursions up and down the Nile on an elaborate gold leaf galley driven by twin banks of oarsmen. In yachtsmen's terms, it was the original "gold plater." (I've seen some opulent powerboats go muttering by and waited in vain for one of them to have *Cleopatra's Barge* emblazoned on the transom.) The magnificently carved Osberg ship was believed to have been built as a pleasure boat for a Norwegian queen sometime around 900 A.D. Going to sea for the sheer pleasure of it seems always to have been a natural thing to do.

There is a difference, though, between going in style and putting out to sea in a very small vessel with few, if any, amenities. Roughing it for fun seems to be a more recent development. It's worth a guess that only since creature comforts became commonplace that going without them has taken on a novel charm. For many who earn their livelihood at sea in small boats, the idea of gratuitous sailing in small boats has seemed odd and a little comical. Still, working sailors were the first to participate in sport sailing—racing.

Getting Somewhere in a Hurry

Getting somewhere in a hurry has long been a Western preoccupation. Cargo vessels paid a premium for fast voyages and some of the great clipper ships competed over courses that took them to markets halfway around the world. As races go, these were without a doubt the most spectacular and thrilling of all time. We will never see their like again.

On a more modest level, fishermen always have competed to be first at the market with their catch. The pressure to develop vessels both rapid and capacious laid the groundwork for modern yachting. Well over a hundred years ago, owners of fishing vessels staged formal races just for the pride and pleasure of seeing whose boat was fastest. It was just a modest jump from those contests to the first yacht races between boats built by private owners—for their pride and pleasure. There it was: the fisherman built his boat to *earn* money with it while the yachtsman earned his money doing something else and got a boat to spend it on. So it has been ever since.

Exploring and Adventuring

When white men first began exploring the North American continent, they rapidly grew to appreciate a traditional native form of watercraft—the canoe. In a country so rich in waterways, the canoe was the ideal vehicle of exploration: light, shallow draft and swift. The canoe rapidly took on a romantic aura and became a powerful symbol as well as a practical vessel. Here was something simple and affordable, not just for the rich but for everyone. With a canoe, one could go exploring, pack a tent and feel a little like Lewis and Clark, Radisson, or even Hiawatha. Soon folks were adapting sailing rigs to canoes and the final ingredient for the modern yachting scene had been added.

What have we got? We have the simple pleasure of just being out on the water . . . we have the pleasures of racing and competition . . . and

A Brief History

we have the pleasures of adventure, of travel, of exploring new places, even if they're only new to us. In one proportion or another these explain what sailors get out of sailing. All of these pleasures are obtainable in small boats. Let's look briefly at some of the highlights of the history of small boat pleasure sailing.

The Birth of Small Boat Cruising

N. H. BISHOP

In 1885 a writer for *Forest and Stream* magazine named N. H. Bishop conceived of the idea of sailing in a tiny sailboat from Pittsburg all the way to the Gulf of Mexico via the Ohio and Mississippi River systems. The vessel he chose was a "sneak box," a small very shallow draft boat originally developed in New Jersey for duck hunting on Barnegat Bay. Nicknamed the "floating coffin" in 1836, the sneak box was fully perfected by Bishop's time. The hull itself was rounded and flat, rather like a spoon. The deck, like the bottom, was rounded too—highly crowned. A daggerboard was mounted well off center to leave the floor clear for a hunter to snuggle down inside the hull for the night. Imagine spending the night *under* your bed and you've got the idea. In such a cramped but nimble vessel Bishop set out for the Gulf. He made it and published the account of his adventures in a book, *Four Months in a Sneak Box*.

SENECA

Bishop's adventures prompted another *Forest and Stream* writer ("Seneca" to his readers) to undertake sneak box voyages of his own. These stories did much to promote public interest in small boat cruising in the United States.

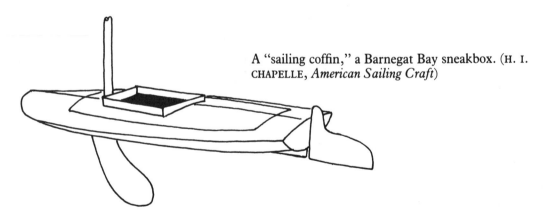

A "sailing coffin," a Barnegat Bay sneakbox. (H. I. CHAPELLE, *American Sailing Craft*)

Coot, South Bay catboat, aboard which C. P. Kunhardt cruised from New York to Beaufort, N.C., and return, 1600 miles, between November, 1885, and July, 1886. (COURTESY INTERNATIONAL MARINE PUBLISHING)

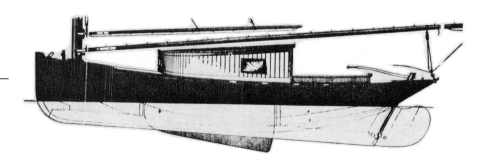

Meanwhile, in England, Robert McMullen was getting the hang of cruising in somewhat larger yachts. It's hard to figure out exactly what pleasures McMullen got out of sailing. Rigid, puritanical, fanatically organized, McMullen seems to have sailed as an exercise in self-discipline. He exasperated even hired crews and, consequently, ended up by necessity pioneering the techniques of sailing singlehanded. By the end of his career he had logged 19,000 miles at sea. He was found dead at the tiller finally while his boat drifted quietly. The year was 1891. McMullen kept careful accounts of his experiences and left a rich legacy of experience for others to follow, hopefully with a lighter heart.

MacGregor

Another Englishman, Captain John MacGregor, disabled from a railway accident, designed a series of light, shallow-draft double enders, which he called "Rob Roy Canoes" and sailed them over one thousand miles through the waters of England, Scandinavia, Europe, and Palestine. His boats, resembling sailing kayaks, gained an instant following after the publication of MacGregor's book *Canoe Travelling* in 1881. Clubs sprang up in England and, in the late 1800's the New York Canoe Club was founded. Rob Roy canoes were easily adapted to racing and soon competition, even between clubs across the Atlantic, became fierce.

The Rob Roy yawl, "The poor man's yacht," under sail. (COURTESY INTERNATIONAL MARINE PUBLISHING)

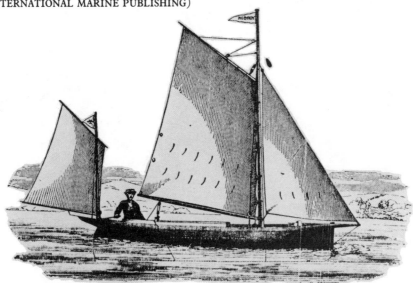

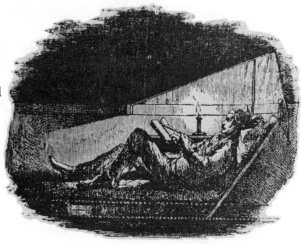

Capt. John MacGregor in his published accounts of cruising on the Rob Roy started a national pastime in motion and added his design concepts to the new field of small boat architecture.

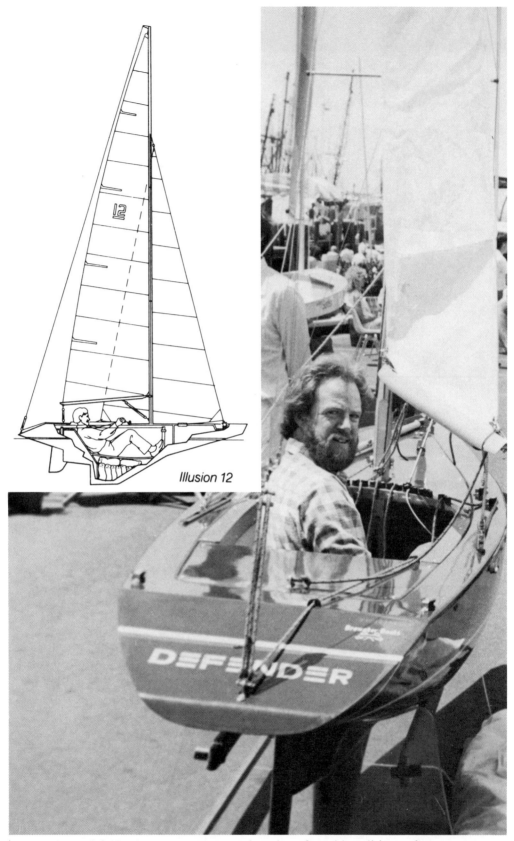

Illusion 12

The modern mini-12 meter racers are a continuation of an old tradition—the racer snuggles down prone inside the hull and steers with his feet.

Still another Englishman, Lt. Middleton, circumnavigated England in a Rob Roy canoe in 1869, inspired by another MacGregor book, *A Thousand Miles in a Rob Roy Canoe*. Middleton then did a rather obvious thing. He began to wonder what it might be like to sail in something just a bit bigger and more comfortable. Remember, there simply weren't any small pleasureboats, with the exception of the Rob Roy, being built anywhere. Middleton adapted a 17-foot fishing boat to his purposes and went on sailing, experimenting and writing. McMullen, MacGregor and Middleton had one thing in common: None of them started off as experienced seamen, nor could they have gotten much sea lore from reading. They were, in fact, "writing the book" themselves.

STRANGE

Picking up where Middleton left off, Alfred Strange, a skilled marine artist as well as sailor and designer, designed a series of compact sailing cruisers. By the time Strange died in 1917, pleasure sailing had taken root in both Europe and America. Many traditional small working craft had been adapted for sailing or for racing, even as the commercial necessity for their existence was passing, and many small builders have preserved the sharpies and dories and traditional catboats—though mostly in fiberglass now. MacGregor, Strange and Middleton all shared the dream that sailing and cruising might be enjoyed, not only by the affluent, but by everybody. In vessels and materials they had never imagined, those dreams have come true.

Alfred Strange 1856–1917 small boat sailor and innovator. (COURTESY INTERNATIONAL MARINE PUBLISHING)

Illustration by Strange of his Cherub II yawl. (COURTESY INTERNATIONAL MARINE PUBLISHING)

TINY OCEAN VOYAGERS
Early Voyagers

Alfred Johnson

Every year or so we read about someone crossing the Atlantic in a tiny six-foot boat. People have been working on that "smallest ever" record for more than a hundred years.

In 1876 Alfred Johnson sailed his 20-foot dory *Centenial* across the Atlantic in a rugged 46-day passage. Centenial Johnson's accomplishment ignited a fervor for small-boat passages. The next year, Thomas Crapo of New Bedford sailed his 19-foot schooner-rigged dory across the Atlantic. He subsequently drowned in 1899 en route from Newport to Cuba in a nine-foot vessel.

In 1880, two gentlemen sailed their 16-foot cutter *Great Western* to England, returning the following year. 1891 saw Josiah Lawlor sail his 15-foot sprit-rigged *Sea Serpent* in a transatlantic race against William Andrews. Andrews' 15-foot gaff sloop capsized and a nearby steamer picked him up. Lawlor made it in 45 days. The following year Andrews did too—in a new boat, the 14-foot *Sapolio*.

(COURTESY INTERNATIONAL MARINE PUBLISHING)

SAILING ON A
MICRO-BUDGET

William Andrews and *Sapolio*.

Modern Micro-voyagers

Clearly small boats can be seaworthy. Nestled down between ocean waves, they often dodge large seas that mercilessly pound larger vessels. However, if caught under a breaking wave, a small boat can be instantly smashed under tons of sea water. Gary Spiess examined the remains of the 11½-foot *Little One* in his book, *Alone Across the Atlantic*. William Willis had perished in *Little One* attempting the voyage Spiess was about to undertake in an even smaller boat.

> "I could see that the *Little One* had suffered a lot of damage. Her mast and boom were gone, a chainplate had been sheared off at the deck and bare wood was exposed in several places where the fiberglass had been torn away. Part of her keel was also broken . . . I stared into the cabin transfixed. Questions crowded my mind. What had happened to Willis? Had he slipped overboard? Had he fallen into such a deep depression that he'd taken his own life? Why hadn't he kept a log—or if he had, why had no one found it? And would *Yankee Girl* and I suffer the same fate?"

Spiess, in his 10-foot boat, survived his 1981 Pacific crossing. Others have not been so fortunate. After successfully crossing two oceans, John Riding and his 12-foot *Sjö Äg* vanished in the Tasmanian Sea.

At this writing, the smallest East-to-West voyager is Eric Peters' five foot, 10 inch sailing "barrel," the *Tonky Nou*. He crossed in 1983 in 46 days. The smallest West-to-East passage was completed in 1983 also, by

A Brief History

Robert Manry nears England after 78 days at sea. (PLAIN DEALER PHOTO BY WILLIAM A. ASHBOLT)

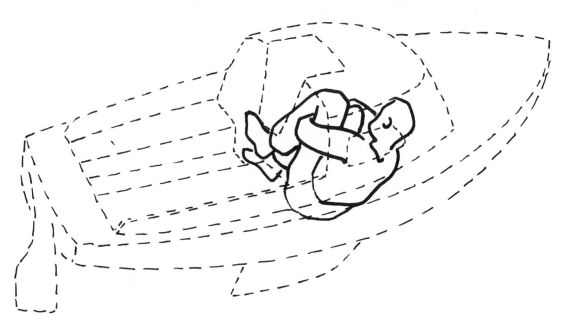

The mariner attempting an epic voyage in an undersized craft can anticipate up to 90 nights curled up like this in a cabin already crammed to overflowing with provisions.

Wayne Dickinson, who sailed his eight foot, 11 inch *God's Tear* across the Atlantic in 142 days to prove, he said, the existence of God.

What is, in fact, proved by all this? Is this cruising? I couldn't and wouldn't want to take anything away from the courage and endurance of these men and the generous courage of their families who also sweated out their passages. But these feats seem to me to have been stunts, tests to tempt destruction of the men and their boats. For the men so tested, the experience surely must be an incredile high. I'm reminded, however, of Robert Manry, who sailed his 13-foot *Tinkerbelle* across the Atlantic in 78 days during the 60's. Suffocating in his job as the classified ads manager for his Cleveland newspaper, Manry modified his family boat and put out to sea. We saw him at last in Falmouth, England, embraced by his family and surrounded by a jubilant throng of well-wishers and admirers. After all this time, I still remember him, arms outstretched, frozen in his moment of triumph. But then what? The boat was crated and shipped home. Manry returned to his desk at the *Plain Dealer*. But how do you return to ordinary living after such an experience?

Questing vs. Cruising

There's a distinction to be made here, subtle but important, between cruising and questing. The cruising sailor who voyages from place to place in a small boat is savoring an experience for its own sake. He, or she, not only enjoys the sail but, upon arrival, lingers to see the sights, meet the people, sample the cuisine. Surely the accomplishment of getting there is a real part of the satisfaction, but only a part. The next cruise could be to anywhere—anywhere at all. But if one's object is to break a record, to generate publicity, *simply to have done it*, then what can be next? One examines the map for a larger body of water, a more dangerous location. Cape Horn. The Arctic. How will it all end?

I like Lin and Larry Pardey's approach. As they left California on their boat someone on the dock called out, "Where are you going?" "We don't know," they replied. "How long will you be gone?" the voice called. "As long as it's fun." I like that.

If you own a small boat or are thinking of getting one, I would urge you not to get swept away by the lure of using it for some epic purpose. Most small boat manufacturers will be the first to tell you that their 17-footer was not designed for extended ocean cruising. You can test your capacity as a sailor to the limit without exceeding the design limitations of your boat while exploring countless rivers, lakes, bays, and seashore coastlines. There are real and deep satisfactions to be found in single-handing, but I would hope they would not, for most sailors, undermine the boat's role as a focal point of *family* adventure and togetherness.

THE LEGENDARY WEST WIGHT POTTER

In 1949 Colin and Stanley Smith built themselves a 20-foot sailboat, *Nova Espero*, in the basement of a chapel in Halifax, Nova Scotia. Being short of money, they lashed a dinghy to the foredeck in lieu of a cabin and set off for England, arriving in 44 days. Two years later, Stanley Smith sailed an improved version across the Atlantic again, in company with Charles Violet, to celebrate the 1951 Festival of Britain.

One can't spend a total of over four months at sea in a small boat without forming some pretty strong opinions about boat design. Stanley Smith settled in England and, on the stormswept Isle of Wight, designed a novel little boat to be built out of plywood. The result was a stout, pug-nosed little vessel only 14 feet long. Her hard-chine hull facilitated her plywood construction and made for a very stiff sailer. Wrote Smith,

> "The high shoulders forward give the boat those few extra inches of free-board just where they are needed to discourage the bow wave from getting carried up by the wind when sailing close-hauled. The lower freeboard in the waist . . . it is at this point where we most frequently get in and out of the boat, where the natural form of the surface of the sea dips down when the boat is moving, and a green sea seldom finds its way on board here. The "kick up" towards the transom, the greater freeboard aft, is very reassuring when contending with awkward following seas. The result is a small craft which feels bigger, more compatible and safer than any other 14 foot boat."

Smith wanted a boat in which one could, for the sheer pleasure of it, venture out into even rough waters and "potter around" as the English would have put it. Smith designed a cabin that contained two six foot, four inch bunks. In fact, the whole floor plan of the cabin was these bunks, divided along part of their length by a centerboard trunk. The cockpit contained a self-bailing footwell. To boost sales, Smith promised to deliver his boats by trailer or by sea, so when an order came in from Sweden requesting water delivery, Smith loaded his tiny boat with provisions, oilskins and warm clothing and, in mid-October, set out across the North Sea. He navigated his way, sometimes through snow, through the Baltic and arrived safe and sound after six weeks at sea. Needless to say, this daring voyage did nothing to diminish either the Potter's or

Stanley Smith on *Nova Espero* before departing for his second transatlantic sail.

Stanley Smith in an early West Wight Potter.

A Potter under sail

Smith's reputation. Soon the vessel was being produced in fiberglass on the American west coast. Smith eventually shut down West Wight Plycraft Co., but by then, the Potter was an established legend.

Some Potter Exploits

In 1970 David Diefenderfer spotted from a plane a city deep in the vast inland swamps and lagoons of east central Mexico. Launching his Potter at the end of an oxcart path near Tuxpan, Diefenderfer penetrated the maze of waterways, eventually spotting a church belfry rising out of the mist. He had found Mexicalititan, an ancient Aztec stronghold. The town boasted, despite its isolation, electricity and even movies. But no tourists. The Potter was the first North American craft to ever penetrate the jungle and possibly the last. Until his death at 80, Diefenderfer's passion was exploring the remote and untraveled waterways of North and Central America. He was planning a trip to Australia when he died.

Drawing only seven inches with its centerboard up, Diefenderfer's boat was ideal for inland odysseys. Still, it was on the high seas that Potters were to make their reputations.

In 1976 David Omick, at the age of 21, accompanied a survey team to Fairbanks, Alaska. Fascinated by the country, he planned a return trip —by boat. Confident that his Potter could survive the trip, Omick set sail from Seattle bound for Ketchikan, 1,000 miles away.

In Queen Charlotte Sound, his little boat was battered by 50-knot winds and 20-foot waves. Twice David was washed overboard only to be swept back to his boat on the next wave. Relying on coastal piloting skills, Omick spent 90 days working his way up the coast, exploring hundreds of scenic inlets and harbors. He is believed to be the first to

The tiny Potters, with the stability of much bigger boats, can track a straight course with the tiller lashed—a great boon to the singlehanded sailor.

have made that rugged passage alone and in so small a boat. Maybe Omick had heard, by then, of John Van Ruth.

Van Ruth, of Tucson, Arizona purchased his Potter in July of 1969. Soon Van Ruth was trying his boat out in the Gulf of California, learning and gaining confidence. Sailing off the Mexican coast again in 1971, Van Ruth was caught in a storm. He writes,

> "The wind picked up the morning of departure, and we tacked all the way to Isla San Esteban. The next day the wind was much stronger so I decided to stay there another day hoping it would diminish; it didn't. Just before sunrise, Freya's anchor broke and we went up on the rocks; somehow I managed to get her off after a nightmare struggle, and hard paddling. I hoisted the jib and got away from the island. Freya was holed on the port side, her rudder was sheared off level with the bottom of the transom and the engine was smashed beyond repair. The outboard bracket was hanging by one arm and the motor was underwater. I kept bailing and I was moving southwest with the current and wind.

> At first I tried to make a rudder out of my paddle by lashing it to the transom. Finally, I got an idea and used the companionway hatch, cutting off the small piece and a crescent section off one corner, then drilling a hole with a whittling knife for the bolt. With little effort I took out the old piece of rudder and bolted the new one on—it worked beautifully. The rest of the trip was a very cold and rough one. I had never been in stronger winds, the tops were blown off the waves and I was soaked for 14 hours or so until we arrived at land."

Convinced that his little boat was safer than a larger yacht, Van Ruth departed from Puerto Vallarta in 1972 and arrived safe and sound in Hilo, Hawaii 80 days later.

> "Freya held up very well. I have cleaned and inspected her hull for cracks but none are present. I was chiefly worried about the ability of the hull to hold up (when close hauled) to oncoming seas and then when she fell into troughs. At one time we hauled continually for five days (short 1 hour) with tiller locked and under main only. She self steers very well close hauled. We made our best day's run of roughly 75 miles . . . I met with no storms but it did become quite rough at times. I honestly believe that sailing a Potter from the Americas to Hawaii is much safer than driving a car the same distance on land."

These voyages differ in one respect from many of the midget ocean crossings that have made the papers: they were actual cruises that were, only incidentally, made in such tiny boats. The navigators had simply used the boats they already owned to go exploring. We pause to look at the West Wight Potter because it represents the first of what eventually became a whole breed of sailboats. After 20 years, the Potter enjoys a continued success in the marketplace, but it is not alone. There are probably at least 40 small sailing cruisers of various kinds on the nation's waterways keeping it company. For the rest of this book, let's look at some of these and consider their applications and their merits.

THE BOATS

PART V

Sailing skiff

In the following section, we're going to take a look at small sailboats suitable for cruising. It's impossible to have an organized discussion about small boats without some system of nomenclature by which boats can be grouped and classified. Clear distinctions are often hard to make, but we'll proceed with the following broad categories:

Micro Cruisers	2 bunks, very lightweight
Compact Cruisers	4 bunks, weight about 1,000 pounds
Family Weekenders	4–5 bunks, the largest boats we'll consider in this book
Open Cruisers	No fixed cabin
Cruising Multi-hulls	Catamarans and small trimarans

We'll also look at boats you can build from kits and boats you can build from scratch or rescue from oblivion as they rot away in boat yards and junkyards. As a potential boat buyer, you have an enormous range of choice.

A TAXONOMY OF SMALL CRUISING YACHTS

MICRO CRUISERS
General Description

A micro cruiser is a small sailboat with a cockpit, an enclosed cabin and two permanent inside berths. These boats are usually 14 to 16 feet long and weigh between 450 and 900 pounds. In such boats, one person can sleep on one berth, stow gear everywhere else and sail astonishing distances in absolutely no comfort at all. Seriously, the long distance mariner is caught in a double whammy with a micro cruiser: Accommodations are minimal and, with such short waterlines, speed is minimal, too. One must thus spend maximum time at sea in a boat offering minimum comforts. But let's face it, most people don't buy these boats to cross oceans in them. Most micro cruisers are purchased to be used as daysailers and many of their owners have never even spent a single night aboard. More's the pity.

A solo sailer can cruise in a micro cruiser for a week with no trouble at all. Two people can sail without replenishing supplies for two or three days if they require no privacy and enjoy camping out on the water. That's what you do in a micro cruiser—you camp out. If you think of the cabin as a permanent fiberglass tent, you'll have the idea.

A family of four can daysail happily and find enough privacy in the cabin to go to the bathroom or wriggle out of wet bathing suits. In most weather, a boom tent or Bimini top can convert the cockpit into a sleeping area for the kids.

In summation, with a micro cruiser, you get really effortless trailering and launching, extended cruising for one, short cruising for two and, with enormous forethought, weekending for a family.

The ideal way to extend the capabilities of this kind of boat is to trailer it from place to place, sailing a day or two here, a day or two there. You can use your car or a van to complement your storage and sleeping accommodations, shop when you need food and otherwise vary the routine. Tents carried aboard can often permit a night or two ashore while you're cruising. You can do more in these boats, I'm sure. People have, but I think you'd be stretching your capacities and the boat's to try to do *too* much more than their designers intended.

Let's look at three of the most popular of the micro cruisers, the West Wight Potter, the Gloucester 16, and the Compac 16.

HMS Marine
904 W. Hyde Park Blvd.
Inglewood, CA 90302

This is the smallest of the three boats we're considering here, only 15 feet long. For most of its history it was 14 feet. It has the smallest cockpit of the three but the most voluminous cabin. Once in the cabin, one sits crosslegged on the bunks. There is no footwell in there. On the contrary, there is a centerboard trunk. It is the only boat of the three with a centerboard trunk intruding into the cabin. There is no ideal place for a head in this boat. One must park the portable toilet in the aft starboard corner of the cabin by day and out in the cockpit at night.

At 475 pounds, the Potter is by far the lightest boat of the three. It is far and away the most lightly ballasted, too, deriving most of its stability from its hard-chine hull shape. Under sail, the Potter heels very little. The mast and rigging seem very light—more like a small daysailer—and one must accept the boat's ultra-light displacement to be satisfied with it.

With its six-inch draft and its low weight, the Potter is very easy to trailer and launch. Esthetically, it's a character boat. Some people are going to find its hard chines and exaggerated sheer odd. Others who like that sort of thing will love their Potters like no other boat they have owned—or will ever own. With the boat's reputation, it's also fun to sail into a new harbor and be asked if you sailed it from England.

The author's Potter, *Fearless*, comes about in a light breeze on the Connecticut River.

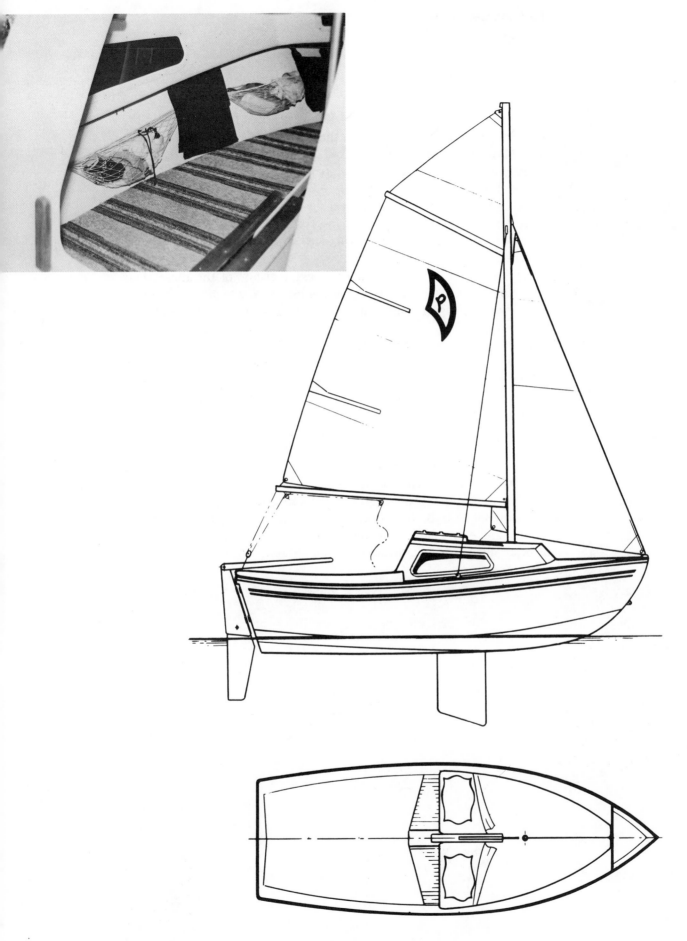

The Gloucester 16

Gloucester Yachts
Box 307
Route 623
Gloucester, VA 23061

Designed some years ago by Bill Lapworth, this boat was called the Newport 16 for many years, then the Lockley Newport 16 for many more. Now the boat is being produced in Virginia. Lapworth is a highly skilled naval architect and his design has, in this case, proved more durable than its manufacturers.

The Gloucester 16 is a swing keel design with a 200-pound centerboard. Stability on this boat derives less from its slippery hull shape than from the influence of the heavy swing keel when its weight is suspended below the hull.

The Gloucester 16 has the largest cockpit of any of the three boats we're looking at. This would be a strong choice of a boat to principally daysail with a gang of folks and for only occasional use overnight with one or two people. The cabin offers two quarterberths with storage space forward. There is a molded-in recess for a head and its central location makes its use a reasonably comfortable proposition. This is nose level for sleeping crew, so it is best removed to the cockpit at night. A filler cushion between the berths is a must. The bunks offer inadequate shoulder and arm room without one. The swing keel is located aft of the cabin, thus a shallow footwell exists between the bunks for sitting out a shower or whatever. The cabin is small, however, and one would want to carefully study the cockpit to see how and where one could store things out there. Cruising on this boat would depend on your skill at adapting some open-boat techniques to using the cockpit. At a total weight of 900 pounds and with nine-inch draft, this too is an extremely portable and easily launchable design. I find the boat looks prettier "in the flesh" than it does in most of the photographs of it I've seen over the years.

During the day, the head lives inside the cabin . . .

. . . but at night it would be at nose level so out it comes into the cockpit.

A Gloucester 16 under sail

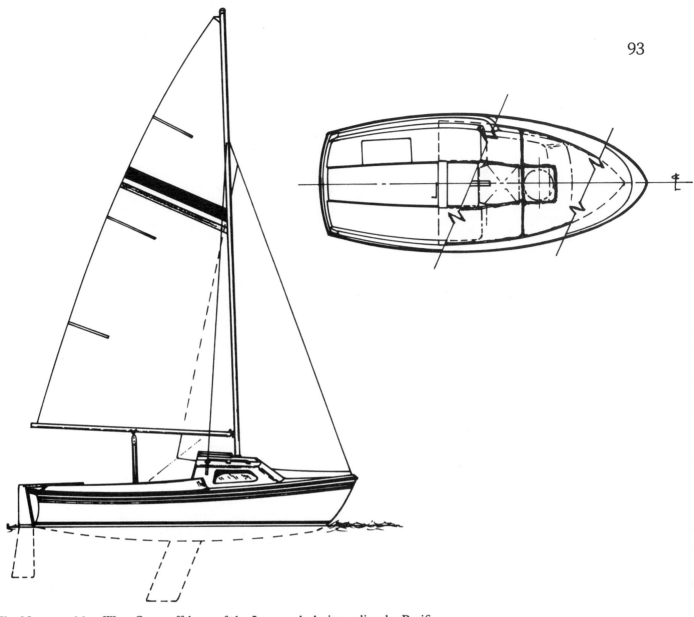

The Neptune 16, a West Coast offshoot of the Lapworth design, plies the Pacific.

The Compac 16

Hutchins Co., Inc.
1195 Kapp Drive
Clearwater, FL 33515

The Compac 16 was designed by Clark Mills, the designer of the Optimist Pram, Sun Cat, and the Windmill, to name a few. Unlike the other two micro cruisers we've looked at, this one is a keel boat with a 450-pound shoal-depth keel. The boat draws 18 inches. Almost all its strengths and weaknesses of the concept derive from this feature.

The Compac's cockpit is certainly adequate for a family of four. There's no centerboard or kick-up rudder to worry about. The shallow keel permits the boat to heel easily at first, then the 450 pounds begin to take effect and the boat stiffens up. The boats' owners seem to find the Compac a handy and able sailer.

Below, the layout of the Compac can be compared to the Gloucester in some ways. It too has two long quarterberths with storage forward. You slide down into the berth with your legs tucked under the cockpit seats. When sleeping, knee room in both boats is limited, as is shoulder room. An insert or a pair of life cushions in the shallow footwell could easily solve the shoulder problem. The forward storage space is generous. You certainly can store your gear and have a place to lie down. Compacs have been written up for some modest cruises. In most cases, the couples involved slept in the cockpits under Bimini tops.

The head storage in the Compac is the best of the three. It fits under the companionway hatch, out of the way. It can easily stay there overnight. For use, it pulls out just a bit and one can sit comfortably with one's head poking out of the hatchway in the fresh air. Not bad.

Weighing 1,100 pounds and drawing roughly a foot more than the other two designs, the Compac 16 is reasonably easy to drag around behind most cars but a bit more difficult to launch. One needs a good ramp. The Compac has a proper "shippy" look to it and it's proved a highly successful design. Several thousand of them have been sold.

These are certainly not the only micro cruisers being sold but they are representative enough so that others can be compared to them easily. All three have been designed by highly competent designers and have stood the test of time and the rigors of the marketplace. Of the three, the Potter is probably the hardest to find used and the Compac the easiest, though I'm speaking from my location on the east coast. The Potter is the only boat of the three produced on the west coast and most Potters are purchased by their owners factory-direct. Being so small, this kind of boat is often a first boat—soon sold in favor of a larger boat. Short of blatant abuse (and careless beaching) these boats should be in fairly good shape when you find them used. They're not all that expensive when you buy them new.

The Compac 16 is a stable boat under sail.

The Compac 16's shallow footwell makes sitting a little more comfortable and also is used as a runway to pull the head out for use —or to stuff it back out of the way under the cockpit.

OTHER MICRO CRUISERS

THE MONTGOMERY 15

Montgomery Marine Inc.
935 W. 18th St.
Costa Mesa, CA 92627

length: 15 feet, draft: 15"/2½'
weight: 750 lbs.

Montgomery boats are tough and very capable sea boats and some impressive sea voyages have been made in a "15" including a 35-day passage from California to Hawaii. The keel/centerboard arrangement provides a fairly comfortable interior with a footwell for sitting down.

The Montgomery 15

THE VICTORIA 18

Sailboat Works Inc.
203 Benson Junction Rd.
DeBary, Florida 32713

length: 18½ feet, draft: 2 feet
weight: 1,200 lbs.

This traditional boat has been around a fairly long time. The slender hull with overhanging stern cuts a graceful figure on the water but makes for narrow bunks and a tight interior. A filler cushion inside, between the bunks, would help.

Check the annual Sail Magazine Boat directory and the various marine magazines' classified sections for listings of additional boats and prices.

The Victoria 18

The buying public seems to want little boats to look like big ones, same shapes, same rigs, just reduced in size. That's a great shame. Actually there's no good reason why a small boat should look just like the big ones and some good reasons why it *should* look different. Certain design opportunities come with reduced size.

I've always been partial to very small boats and have given a lot of thought to their design. If I had carte blanche to design my own micro cruiser, here's how it would look:

1. The hull would resemble, in many ways, a West Wight Potter. I like stability and shallow draft in a small boat. I would have the hull lapstrake from the chine up. Why? First of all because I've always liked how it looks. The corrugated effect you get when you mold lapstrakes to fiberglass adds great stiffness, which is nice to have in a light hull. Finally, the strakes tend to reduce spray and make for a drier ride. The Potter is already quite dry; this boat would be even drier, if that's possible.

2. Fifteen feet isn't a bad size. I'd raise the cockpit coamings in the stern of the boat from the modern Potter. Older Potters had more freeboard aft. A bit stodgy by modern tastes, but it made for a safer sea boat and I guess I'm old-fashioned.

3. In a boat as tiny as a micro cruiser, I'd want to get rid of the centerboard trunk inside the cabin. A small footwell—as in the Compac 16 or the Montgomery 15—would be handy. On the other hand, I would still want a beachable boat. There is a solution, which Drascombe boats use successfully. I would enlarge the Potter's small keel. I'd make it wider and about three inches deeper. Concrete could be poured in for ballast during construction. I would also glass on two bilge keels to the bottom. The surface area of all three keels would equal or exceed that of a centerboard. The boat would still draw something like 10 or 12 inches, even sailing to windward. No boat in existence today can do that. The bilge keels would stiffen the hull and permit stable beaching. This system has been proven. It awaits a manufacturer with the courage to market it and the skill to sell the concept along with the product.

Lapstrake in fiberglass: The corrugations add great strength with no penalty in weight.

For strength and spray reduction: lapstrake from chine to gunwale.

Tri keels: One skeg and two bilge keels.

4. The sail rig would reflect all we have learned (especially from Garry Hoyt) about modern cat rig design. The fully battened sail would offer good drive and easy reefing. The shape would permit deep reefing without unbalancing the boat. The sail, you'll notice, lacks a boom. The bottom sail panel would keep the sail from twisting out of shape and, in addition, offer no hazard to those in the cockpit. Little boats are often people's first boats. People make mistakes when learning and a short aluminum boom can sweep the cockpit with near-lethal force. The horizontal battens permit the sail to be dropped easily, too. The rig is a little strange-looking, I'll admit, but it has enormous virtues. Short rigs tend to make a boat heel less, another plus. I'd squirt a plug of flotation foam into either end of the hollow mast, too. That would deaden sound and make the mast buoyant, protecting the boat from capsize. Small blocks of foam would also be sewn into the head of the sail on both sides to further aid in recovery in the unlikely event of a knockdown. I know from experience that a Potter (even with its centerboard up) will snap back on its feet from a 90-degree knockdown. Masthead flotation would guarantee that any knockdown would be no more than 90 degrees. I like extra margins.

Well, there you have it. A very seaworthy, very shallow draft, go-anywhere boat. You'd have an unobstructed cabin with room to sit and room for a happy couple to snuggle. It has a simple, handy and efficient sail rig, an unobstructed foredeck where the kids could sit without a jib flapping in their faces—an ideal tiny boat. I hope somebody will make one.

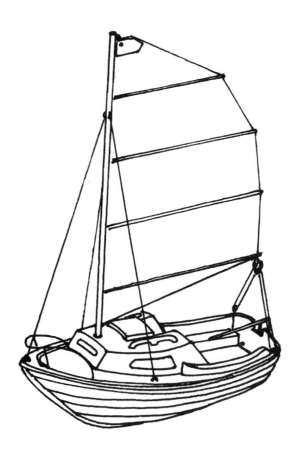

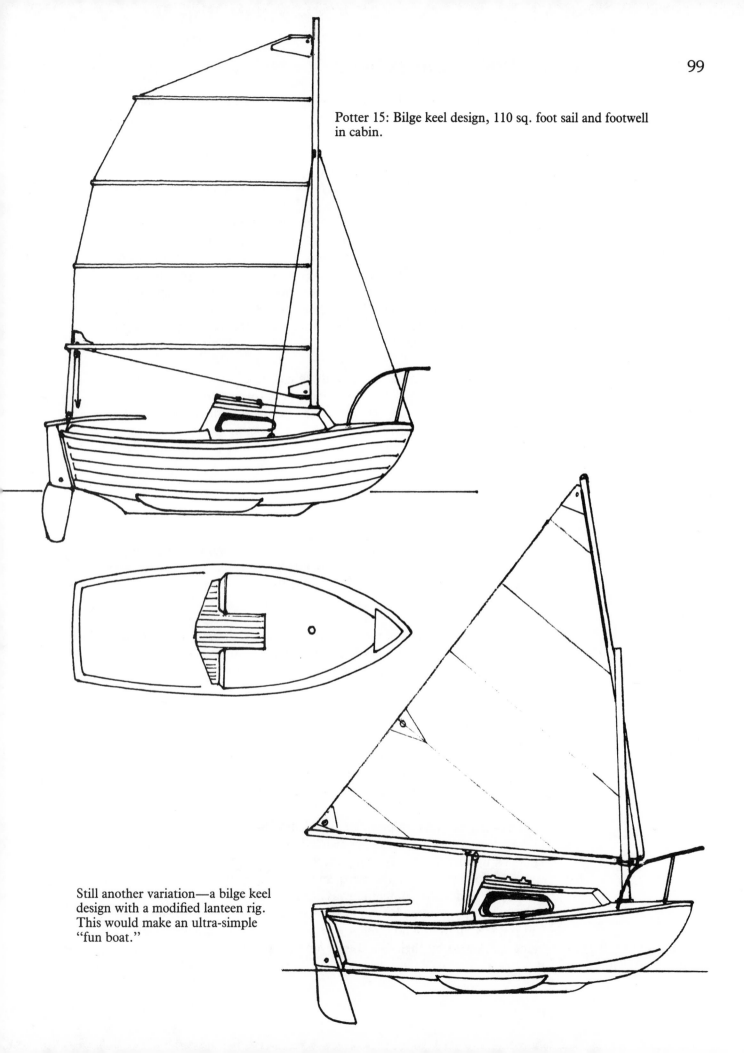

Potter 15: Bilge keel design, 110 sq. foot sail and footwell in cabin.

Still another variation—a bilge keel design with a modified lanteen rig. This would make an ultra-simple "fun boat."

Compact cruisers are sailboats with cockpits, enclosed cabins and up to four permanent inside berths. Such boats are usually 17 to 20 feet long and weigh between 1,000 and 2,000 pounds.

In compact cruisers, one person can cruise in resonable comfort for extended distances. Tristan Jones actually lived aboard his 19-foot *Sea Dart*. Shane Acton sailed his 18-foot *Super Shrimp* around the world with a companion.

Two people can, in most compact production boats, cruise up to a week—sometimes much longer. But when a family of four piles into a compact cruiser, space is at a premium. There is room to crouch in the cabin but floor space is minimal and everyone shouldn't expect to stand up at once. Especially if more than two people expect to sleep in the cabin, use of monkey hammocks and pouches attached to the cabin walls is a must. Storage under the berths—especially the vee berth—begins to help in boats this size but this is still minimal cruising and should be approached as such.

A family of four can daysail happily in a compact but the investment (half again to twice the cost of a micro) is hardly worth it unless you really plan to put the compact's superior interior volume to use.

In summation, a compact cruiser offers voyaging potential for one, comfortable week-long cruising for two, weekending for four, and daysailing in fine weather for up to six.

Interiors

Almost all commercially-made compacts offer accommodations based on the vee and double quarterberth layout. Room is limited so space for a head or a galley is cramped. There's really little design freedom in boats this small.

Some boats in this class offer galleys—often with tiny bowl-shaped sinks. Many such sinks are too small to hold even a dinner plate and the first motorboat that passes sloshes the contents of the sink all over the galley. A hole cut in the countertop for a standard plastic bucket would be better. Dishes could be stored down there under way (without falling out) to be washed later. A little soapy water can even be allowed to slosh back and forth over them under way. The bucket itself is stored neatly, too. Buckets are handy on boats but there's never a place to put them. In many compacts, cooking is best done in the cockpit. Just because everyone has an inside berth, don't overlook the cockpit. A boom tent or a Bimini can turn the cockpit into a comfortable living room and add enormously to comfort afloat.

Most compacts have a permanent spot for the head. Beware of heads located way up in the peak. In many light boats, motion is very pronounced up there; space is cramped, ventilation may be poor. Someone could go forward to use the head and wind up getting sick. A better location is under the companionway. One thing you've probably gathered by now, you can't be proud on a small boat. It's best to just grin and relax. Children, who often are going through an annoying phase of being fascinated by their—and everyone's—bodily functions, will find this casual intimacy hilarious at first and then will relax. Bathroom jokes will die down; you may grow to enjoy your kids better. Remember to thank your boat.

Some compact cruisers are designed expressly for two occupants. Most small catboats, for example, have only two bunks below. For cruising couples, this makes good sense—two really comfortable bunks and adequate storage lockers. More companies should offer a choice of interiors, one with four berths, one with only two.

Let's look at a typical compact cruiser to get an overall impression of the type, and then let's look at some specific features of several other boats that bear scrutiny.

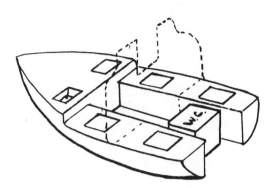

Vee and two quarter berths. W.C. (potti) under bridgedeck Skipper 20, Skipper's Mate . . . Holder 20 and 17 Sovreign 17 . . . O'Day Mariner . . . Compac 19 . . . Mirage 18 . . . Slipper 17 . . . Venture 17 . . . Starwind 19

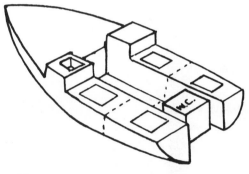

Vee berth, split galley, quarterberths. MacGregor 21 . . . Montego 19 and 20 . . . Gloucester 19 and 20 . . . Freedom 21

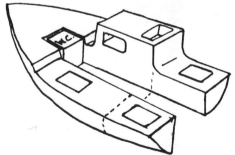

Vee berth, single quarterberth, linear galley (head locations vary). Montgomery 17 . . . Sovreign 17.

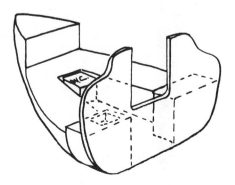

Two single berths, split galley aft: Boston Whaler 6.2 . . . Harpoon . . . Mystic Cat and sloop . . . Marshall 18 Catboat . . . Cape Cod Shipbuilders Catboat . . . Nauset Marine Cat . . . Drascombe's Coaster and Drifter . . . Ranger 20.

The Boats

The Skipper's Mate*

The Skipper's Mate was designed by naval architect Charles Ludwig, who designed her as a centerboard sloop. He neatly solved the intrusion of a centerboard well into the cabin by mounting the board off the boat's centerline and incorporating the trunk into one of the quarterberths. An open footwell (a usual keelboat advantage) graces the cabin and the toilet slides away under the companionway hatch.

The vee berth is very roomy and one of the quarterberths, the one incorporating the centerboard trunk, is enormous. Kneeroom under the cockpit seats is just adequate though. There is storage and space for a stove under a set of cushions at the end of the vee berth—a nice compromise assuming you're not going to cook and go to bed at the same time. Opening ports afford good ventilation in the cabin, should you wish to cook in there.

With the centerboard up, the Skipper's Mate draws only 12 inches, giving it easy beachability and a shallow-water potential shared by few other boats.

With the Mate's seven-foot beam, the cockpit is both long and roomy. There's space to stretch out in it and a boom tent or a Bimini top would add still another dimension to the boat's comfort. With a jaunty traditional appearance, the boat is an appealing, no-nonsense approach to inexpensive family cruising with few faults and almost all the virtues one would hope to find in a compact cruiser.

Southern Sails Inc., the builder, is a small, relatively new concern at this writing. There won't be many of these boats around used for a while. The new boats are reasonably priced though and you get a 1,200-pound boat that's easily trailered, launched and sailed.

* Just prior to press time, the molds for The Skipper's Mate were sold to Captiva Yachts, 4501 Ulmerton Road, Clearwater, FL 33520. The name has been changed to The Sanibel 17.

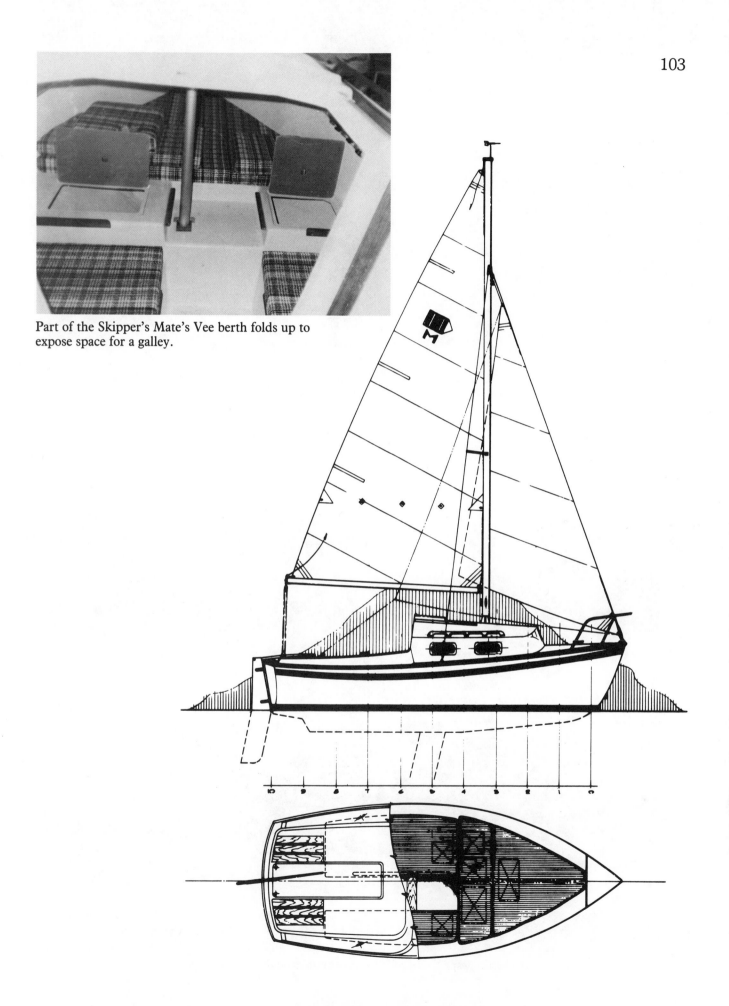

Part of the Skipper's Mate's Vee berth folds up to expose space for a galley.

Sovereign 17 underway. Note short bowsprit with roller to assist raising and stowing anchor.

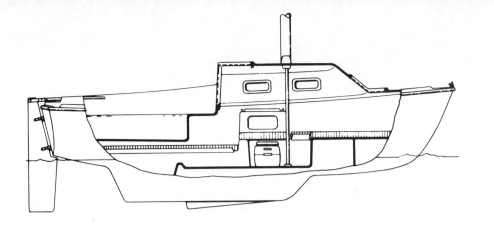

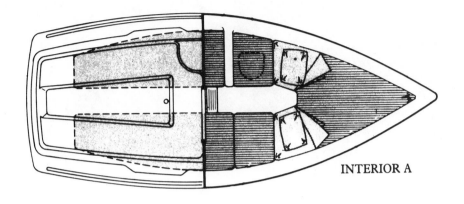

INTERIOR A

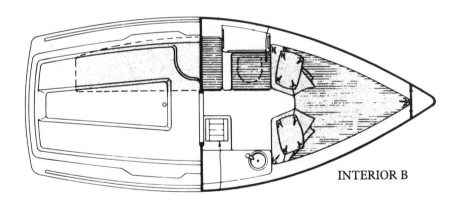

INTERIOR B

Sovereign 17

Sovereign Yachts
233 Commerce Dr. S.
Largo, FL 33540

   This boat's accommodations are, for a cruising couple, almost elegant. The head is tucked out of sight under a seat off to one side and there is a small but serviceable galley built into the hull liner. A table can be mounted to the mast support post, another nice touch, and the vee berth is full-sized and comfortable. The Sovereign, like the Skipper's Mate, has opening ports to ventilate the cabin plus a forward hatch. Sovereign offers, for a lower price, the same hull with an interior layout similar to that of the Skipper's Mate. More companies should offer interior options like that.

The Boats

The Marshall Sanderling (PHOTO BY NORMAN FORTIER)

Marshall Marine
P.O. Box 266
South Dartmouth, MA 02748

Let's look at the traditional interior of a Cape Cod catboat. This one is built by Marshall Shipyard in South Dartmouth, Mass. Here you've got only two berths—all a couple needs—and a small galley. The head is forward. It makes sense, if you're a couple, to get an interior with only a couple of bunks. You can really move into the interior of such a boat. I met a young couple in Newport happily *living* aboard a catboat only 20 feet long. An awning shaded the cockpit. Laundry hung drying from the boom and shrouds. It was summer and they had all they needed. Another forty thousand dollars would have bought them only more worries.

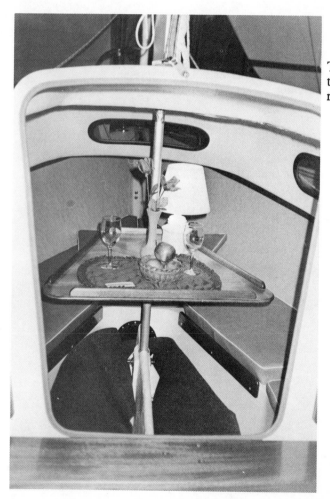

The Siren has no built-in galley unit. It does have a clever table arrangement that drops to enlarge the Vee berth or raises to the overhead out of the way when not in use.

With its 8-foot beam, The Slipper offers the interior volume of many larger boats.

The Slipper 17 has an asymmetrical interior with a sink unit on the port side.

Montego 19 and 20

Universal Marine
1421 Bay St. SE
St. Petersburg, FL 33701

Montego makes a boat sold as the "19" or the "20," depending on whether you're buying a swing keel or a skeg keel version. You have a choice. In the interior of both boats, the vee and the quarterberths are separated by a pair of cabinets. A bowl-like sink is molded into the top of one of the cabinets; a stove can be mounted on the counter opposite. Now these little sinks are as much cosmetic as functional. You could cut out a larger hole and sink a bucket in there and really have something. Still, *any* additional storage and counter space—even divided—is a help. In a boat longer than the Skipper's Mate or the Sovreign, the split counter is a reasonable design decision.

The split galley on the Montego 20. Note the oversized hatchway, offering generous standing room in the cabin.

A Montego 20 under sail.

OTHER COMPACT CRUISERS

THE SIREN 17

Vandestadt & McGruer Ltd.
Box 7
Owen Sound, Ontario
Canada N4 K5P1

length: 17′ 2″, draft: 8″/4¼′
weight: 750 lbs.

You'll find a lot of these boats on the east coast. This centerboarder has a simple but flexible cabin interior and an elaborate boomtent as a factory option that turns the cockpit into a roomy second cabin.

The Siren 17

The MacGregor 21

MACGREGOR 21

MacGregor Yacht Corp.
1631 Placentia
Costa Mesa, CA 92627

length: 21 feet, draft: 1 ′ to 5½′
weight: 1,000 lbs.

MacGregor has made almost five thousand of these boats; they're good buys new or used. The 21 is light for its length and is *very* fast under sail. Being light, the boat is easily trailered; being a little longer than most compacts, the 21 has more storage space. It's a very pretty boat too.

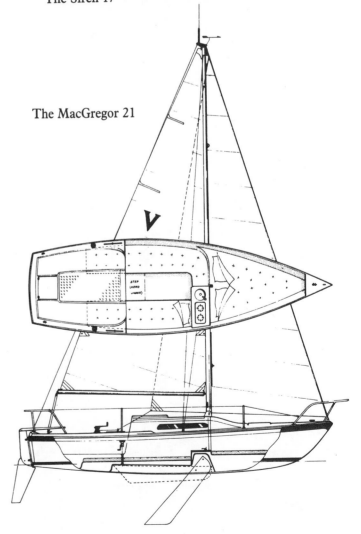

THE SKIPPER 20

Southern Sails Inc.
4477 K. 122nd Avenue
N. Clearwater, FL 33030

length: 18', draft: 2'
weight: 2,000 lbs.

Here's a boat with unique character. The double-ended lapstrake hull has a Scandinavian appeal. There's an outboard well tucked neatly away in the stern too. The shoal keel leaves the interior open; an extra large hatchway provides good standing room. Massively constructed.

The Skipper 20

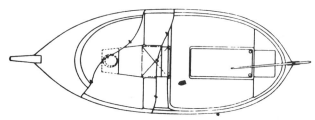

The Holder 20

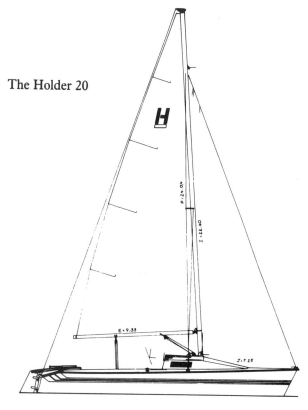

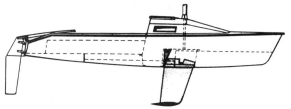

HOLDER 20

Hobie Cat
Box 1008
Oceanside, CA 92054

length: 20¼', draft: 3' 7"
weight: 1,160 lbs.

Here is another very fast boat, possibly faster than the MacGregor 21. The drop keel eliminates the drag of a centerboard trunk cavity. It winches up for trailering. The interior is a simple vee and two quarterberth layout.

THE GLOUCESTER 20

Gloucester Yachts
Box 307
Route 623
Gloucester, VA 23061

length: 19½′, draft: 1 to 4′
weight: 1,500 lbs.

The Gloucester 20 is an attractive boat with a nice blend of contemporary and traditional lines. The interior is roomy with fairly large quarterberths and a split galley. The boat is also available with a fixed keel.

Check the annual Sail Magazine Boat Directory and the various marine magazines' classified sections for listings of additional boats and prices.

The Gloucester 20

There's an enormous variety of compact cruisers to choose from. They show up used frequently, too. You certainly have more weight to lug around. When buying used, be sure the *trailer* has held up at least as well as the boat. Owners often totally neglect the trailers their boats sit and ride around on.

I'd say if there is a single difference that separates the compact from the micro cruiser, it is that one camps out on a micro cruiser and one begins to actually live (if only briefly) in the cabin of a compact cruiser. Before trading up from a compact to anything bigger, I would want to make sure I had made full use of the *cockpit* as well as the cabin first. For many sailors, a properly outfitted compact cruiser is all the boat they might ever need.

FAMILY WEEKENDERS

The largest type of small sailboats we'll look at are family weekenders, sailboats 20 to 25 feet in length. They are designed to offer the maximum accommodations within the weight limitations imposed by trailering and ramp launching with the family car. Thus, they tend to be relatively light for their size, between 2,000 and 2,500 pounds. Family weekenders are not designed as offshore cruisers and their manufacturers would be the first to discourage you from planning, say an Atlantic crossing, in one. On the other hand, two people could cruise in more protected waters almost indefinitely or even live aboard if their boat had a pop-top for standing headroom. A family can easily go on a long weekend—or longer—in comfort.

Most family weekenders do offer pop-tops. Being able to pull your pants on standing up is nothing to sneer at. In reasonable weather, you can sail with the top up, turning your cabin into an airy and pleasant extension of the cockpit. Most of these boats also have optional galley units, a "private" space for the head, and often a table that makes into a double bunk at night.

The family weekender is trailerable behind a full-size car, but realistically, this is not a towing job for a compact automobile. A larger domestic car will handle one of these boats nicely on the interstate. In rural mountainous country, you need a muscle vehicle. If a lot of serious overland travel is going to be part of your vacation pattern, a micro or compact cruiser will be more suitable. If your overland travel is more modest, the comforts offered by this kind of boat make it very tempting. There are a number of boats of this kind available. Let's compare in detail two family weekenders that offer distinctly different approaches.

1631 Placentia
Costa Mesa, CA 92627

This boat is one of a series of boats offered by MacGregor yachts out of California. When I was considering purchasing one for my own use, I was warned away by many yachtsmen whose opinions I respected. "They're too light . . . They're cheap and cheaply made . . . You get what you pay for . . ." and so on. After all, the MacGregor 22 was the cheapest boat of its size money could buy. How could it be any good?

Then I started interviewing people at launching ramps and folks I met afloat who owned MacGregors. They were all happy as clams. After a lot of study—and on a short budget—I got a "22." I called the boat the *2nd Wind* and sailed it hard and often for two years. My wife and two daughters practically lived on it for a whole summer. Here's what you get:

The MacGregor 22

The boat has a sleek modern appearance. My tastes are more traditional but it was a fine-looking boat. The boat is very light. Not weak, I've decided, but very light. The deck flexes when you walk on it and that takes some getting used to. Yet the boat can be slammed around on Buzzard's Bay or out in the ocean and nothing breaks. I suspect this is a boat that can stand use better than abuse. You shouldn't wait to reef when it's time. I wouldn't jump down on the foredeck from too great a height, either. White-water kayaks flex if you shove your fist against them, yet they bounce off rocks and absorb incredible punishment. MacGregor has gone the kayak route with a cruising sailboat. This is an unconventional approach and I guess there will always be doubts and criticism. Meanwhile thousands of people go sailing on these boats.

The MacGregor 22 is a swing keel design. The 500-pound keel offers a lot of stability when it's down. When it's up, the boat can sneak into as little as 12 inches of water. The extreme shallow draft is an endearing feature. The 22 can plane downwind and do a creditable job upwind. To my surprise, I found I could lash the helm and let the boat sail itself when going upwind. That's a huge relief. There is a point, when the wind and waves get nasty enough, when plowing to windward is too much trouble for what you get out of it. It is, after all, a lightweight boat. A four-horsepower outboard is sufficient to move it around nicely, though.

One area where there is little compromising is below. The cabin is very basic but very liveable. The vee berth forward is a generous space for two kids. If you move the toilet into the aisle, the private head compartment can be turned into a huge storage area. From the wooden molding that runs around the liner/deck joint inside the cabin, monkey hammocks, canvas pouches, towel racks, etc. can be hung, putting all that space to good use and keeping stuff off the seats and beds. The

The MacGregor 22. Note the pop-top.

table is big enough to seat four people, or to sleep a couple of adults in reasonable comfort.

The MacGregor 22 is a flush deck design. There is no raised cabin trunk with narrow walk-around decks. The flush deck is not only easier to manufacture, it offers more interior space. On the other hand, the flush deck makes going forward underway a tricky proposition—especially for children. Even with extra handrails bolted on at strategic points, when the boat is heeling over and the decks are slick with spray, a flush deck is a hairy place to move around. With the pop-top up in milder weather, you can gain the foredeck via the cabin, even reach the mainsail halyards while standing inside the boat.

The pop-top is the single feature that most transforms the cabin into a real living space. A large canvas "dodger" fits over it and snaps to the cabin roof. We found it to be semi-waterproof, not up to a continual downpour without leaking. Still, the system was a valuable addition, even though often the times you need the space most is when it's raining cats and dogs.

The Boats

The area under the cockpit seats is very generous. There's room for extra water bottles, a solar shower, life jackets, fenders, line, a spare anchor, guitar, skin diving gear—all sorts of things. More space was available under the seats in the cabin. Water does find its way in here occasionally. It's advisable to buy a bunch of those plastic racks you put dishes into after washing them. You can line your locker bottoms with them and they'll keep the inch of water that sloshes around down there from soaking your gear.

The cockpit is big enough to easily accommodate a family of four. Early designs years ago put the centerboard winch out in the cockpit. They got rusty and ugly out there so MacGregor moved them inside the cabin. Ugly or not, I prefer to have the centerboard controls out where the sailing is going on.

In sum, you get a lot of cruising for your money. When you buy a boat, you're buying fiberglass by the pound. Boat cost will often have more to do with hull *weight* than it will with boat length. Although such

Note the winch handle for the centerboard under the companionway watch in this MacGregor 22 . . .

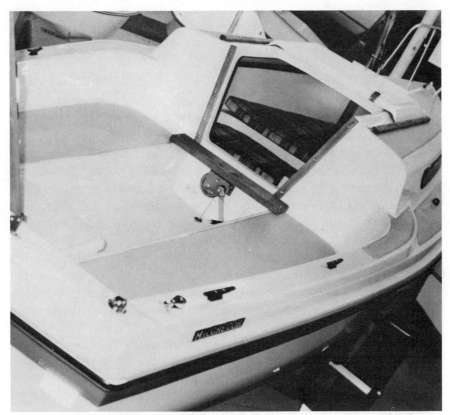

. . . The proper place for it is out in the cockpit where the actual sailing is taking place. Now, in foul weather, you can close up the cabin and still have control over your draft as in this MacGregor 21.

a light boat must have its limitations, these are not limitations usually reached by the average family. We had a whole lot of fun with *2nd Wind*.

When I moved with my family from the seacoast to Vermont, I was still paying off the boat loan. We needed the money. The 22 was also too much to haul up and down over the mountains of Vermont. Our needs had changed and so, with no hard feelings, we parted company with *2nd Wind* and bought a West Wight Potter. We're going a totally different route now.

MacGregors are, foot for foot, the most inexpensive new boats you can buy. If you can buy anything—especially a small boat—without financing, try to do it. We found the monthly payment for the boat coming out of the same budget our vacation money came from. If you made the same discovery, you'd find that the boat was beginning to own you . . . and we've already talked about that one. Used MacGregors are plentiful because they sell so many boats. Selling a MacGregor can be an exercise in humility because your boat competes on the used market-place with several other older and cheaper boats of the same model. It's probably not the best idea to expect to get top dollar on *any* small boat you sell. Price it to move and let it go. Then you can get on with whatever you plan to do next. Buying a used MacGregor can be a good way to see how differently people can customize the same boat. Check the drop keel area to make sure it's in good shape. Check the places where stress is applied to local areas, chainplates, cleats, lifelines. Any evidence of putty might suggest some carelessness along the line. You can, at a good price, often get a boat *fully equipped*. That represents a huge savings.

The Boats

The O'Day 22

Bangor Punta Marine
848 Airport Road
Box 991
Fall River, MA 02722

The O'Day 22 is one of a highly successful series of designs by Raymond Hunt and Associates. If you crawl under an O'Day 22, you'll notice one of Hunt's innovations. Despite the soft turn of the bilges, the O'Day 22 has a flat bottom. It doesn't look like a flat bottom boat sitting in the water, but it is. Whereas the MacGregor depends on its drop keel for a good measure of its stability, this design gets a good deal of initial stability from its shape. The O'Day has a keel/centerboard. The ballast on this boat is in the keel; the centerboard is fiberglass and is useful only to improve windward performance. Given its great weight, nothing impedes the MacGregor centerboard from dropping out of its trunk when lowered away. The lighter O'Day board can get stuck if barnacles and seaweed are allowed to grow inside the trunk. It's worth checking the marine growth in the trunk from time to time. With a keel/centerboard, you have no mechanical parts inside the hull. The pivot pin is in the keel. This arrangement doesn't leak into the cabin and the lightweight board can be pulled up and down with a simple lanyard. On the other hand, running aground with a swing keel boat consists of coming to a stop when its cast-iron keel runs into something. Running aground in a keel centerboarder increases the likelihood that you're going to bounce your fiberglass keel off something. You're going to have to be more careful.

The O'Day's cockpit feels deeper than the MacGregor's. You're down in it more. The O'Day 22 has a trunk cabin with grab rails running along both sides. This arrangement gives you walk-around decks and a way to move forward on the boat with greater safety and security. There is no pop-top. You have more headroom than the MacGregor with its top

The O'Day under sail. A transparent panel in the jib improves forward visibility.

The O'Day 22 has a somewhat deeper cockpit than the MacGregor. Note handrails on the cabin top.

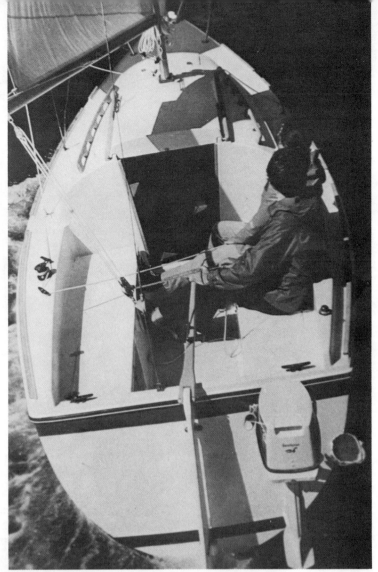

Looking below into the O'Day 22.

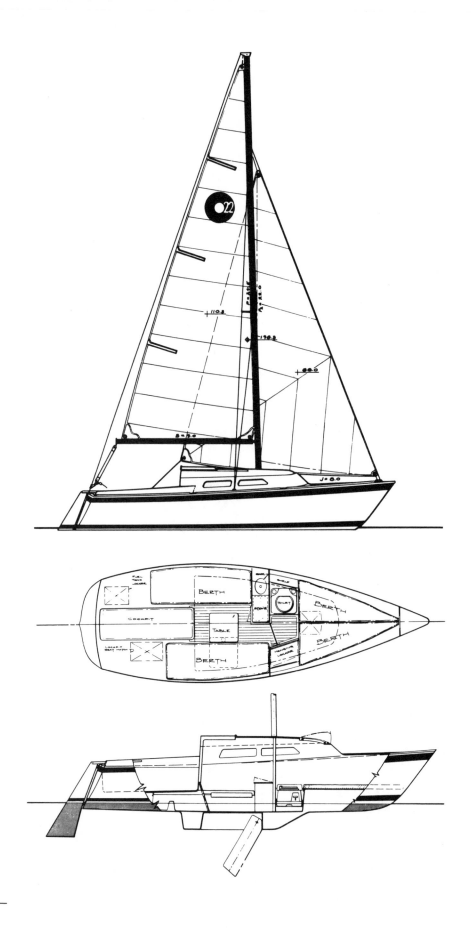

down, less than with its top up. The ventilation provided by the forward hatch is crucial. As on the MacGregor, there are no opening ports.

Construction on the O'Day 22 is heavier. When you rap your knuckles on the O'Day's hull below the waterline, it's like knocking on a sidewalk. The highly crowned cabin adds strength, too. I've never seen a MacGregor that's fallen apart, but the O'Day *feels* stronger and some people are going to be attracted by that.

Down below, the cabin layout takes a different approach from the MacGregor. The MacGregor's interior is largely dictated by the intrusion of the centerboard trunk. The table/bunk setup is comfortable and useful; it was also a design necessity.

The O'Day has an open central floor. A table can be set up in the cabin or taken down and put completely away. Two generous quarterberths sleep the adults. Forward, a vee berth sleeps the kids. A midcabin bulkhead separates the two sleeping areas. The head hides around the corner on the forward side of the bulkhead; a galley is set up on the after side. The whole interior has a traditional shippy feel to it.

At 2,500 pounds and drawing 15 inches with the board up, the O'Day is a bit harder to handle on the highway. I've met fewer people who trailer O'Day's, but many launch their own boat in the beginning of the season and then retrieve it again in the fall. Many of these boats winter in their owners' backyards.

Used O'Day's show up a lot. Older versions of the 22 had a skeg keel drawing two feet. O'Day also made a 20-foot boat almost identical to the 22. It was a good boat.

I would recommend buying your used boats from private individuals and selling your used boat privately. The dealer has to charge a commission. That's how he lives. But that commission either eats into my profits or forces me to raise the price. The private seller can offer his boat for sale at a lower price. No one can sell your boat more enthusiastically and compellingly than you can. When you buy, you can size up the owner and figure out what kind of care was taken of the boat, where it was used and so on.

Summary

There is no right or wrong answer to design questions—only personal preferences. Pop-top or not; centerboard or keel; flush deck or trunk cabin; table/double or twin berths; lightweight or heavier. The choices must reflect your needs, your budget. Of all the boats we will cover within the scope of this book, family weekenders represent the most living space, the greatest comfort, and the most serious financial investment. Naturally the size and cost of yachts goes onward and upward, but that is not our concern here. To the contrary, I would warn only that we are at the threshold of the point where our commitments of time and money and care begin to lead us around by the nose. So long as you own it rather than it own you, you're all right. If you can barely afford a family weekender, don't get one. Go down one size and own it outright; be carefree. If the price is not a source of worry, what the hell. Splurge!

A lot of interior can fit into 22 feet of boat. Here, the Spindrift 22 offers a split galley and a table that folds out from the centerboard trunk.

THE CATALINA 22

Catalina Yachts
21200 Victory Blvd.
Woodland Hills, CA 91367

length: 22', draft: 20" to 3½'
weight: 2,200 lbs.

More than 11,000 of these boats have been
manufactured over the years. The interior of the
Catalina 22 is similar to that of the MacGregor 22. The
swing keel is housed largely outside the hull acting,
when raised, almost like a shoal keel. Pop top offered.

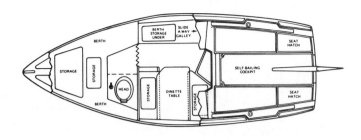

THE MACGREGOR 25

MacGregor Yachts Inc.
1631 Placentia Ave.
Costa Mesa, CA 92627

length: 25', draft: 18" to 5'
weight: 2,400 lbs.

The MacGregor 25, though longer than most boats we're considering, is within the weight and cost ballpark. MacGregor builds lightweight hulls. The 25 is laid out much like the 22, with just more head and elbow room all around. With the pop top, headroom is 6 feet, 2 inches. More than 9,000 boats have been built, providing for a brisk used boat market.

Here you get a clear indication of the live-aboard possibilities of a family weekender.

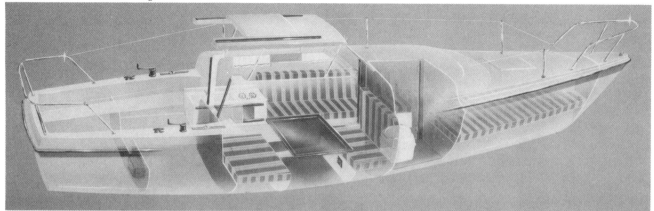

The MacGregor 25

If you're short on cash, you've probably paid special attention to ads about boat kits and boat plans. Maybe you've had ideas about getting your hands on an old lifeboat or a dory and fixing it up or turning it into an inexpensive yacht. What about that?

There's an old saying that runs something like this: "Before you start building the boat that will take you around the world, see if you can build the dinghy for it first." If you hate building the dinghy or, worse still, if you *can't* build it, then you've learned an invaluable lesson and paid for it cheaply. Building your own boat has a variety of meanings. Let's consider each in turn.

Fiberglass Boat Kits

There are a number of companies in the marketplace offering boats in various stages of completion. Luger Boats in the midwest seems to be the largest outfit of this kind, so let's look at their approach for a moment.

When you buy a Luger kit, the hull and the deck/cabin sections come to you already joined and connected in several spots. The builder (you) completes the process by glassing hull and deck together with strips of glass cloth soaked in resin. Wooden floor supports are glassed in and then the cabin interior is fabricated in plywood and glassed into place. The plywood can be purchased locally or you can purchase the pieces already cut out from the factory.

The keel assembly is bolted in place; sailing gear is bolted in, motor mount, etc. and eventually it's all done. You've done it yourself and you've saved some money.

Advantages are several: If you're a good craftsman, the interior can be built to yacht standards. You can add as much reinforcement to the hull as you want as you build in—even overbuild it if you want. You have the advantage of knowing almost everything there is to know about your boat once you're done. On the other hand, if you are not a good and thorough craftsman, the interior of your boat may end up looking crude and amateurish. Should you wish to sell the boat later, you'll take a beating. If you've taken too many shortcuts, or if you're simply not a craftsman at all, your boat might actually be unsafe. In the event of a serious failure, someone could be injured or worse, or you might be left with a boat impossible to sell at any price. It's all on your shoulders when you build it yourself.

I will suggest only one really good reason exists for building a boat yourself: not because you'll save money; not so you can brag to your bedazzled guests that you built her yourself. The only good reason is you really want to do your own work. Greed or pride won't do. If you really are turned on by the idea of building a boat from scratch or from a kit, then you'll probably do a fair job of it and be content with the result. The kits themselves are all right; I don't want to imply otherwise. The issue isn't the boat but the builder. If you aren't an experienced craftsman, consider not only what what you might save, but what you might lose if you bungle the job.

The Boats

Luger's 21-foot kit boat.

Everything I've said about kit boats applies doubly here. Only do it if you're sure you'll love the process even more than the product. There are many innovative and appealing ideas out there for those who want to work. Consider getting someone else to fabricate a small boat for you and compare the cost to a production boat. If you've fallen in love with a design, it may make sense to do it that way if you're not a good craftsman. You can personally monitor progress, suggest new ideas, and get involved sawing, sanding and painting if you feel like it. The end result will feel very personal and very special.

Buying A Semi-finished Production Boat

See if the manufacturer of a boat you like will sell you a boat only partially finished. The degree of incompletion is up to you. You might catch him during a slow time in December and the builder might flex with you. You could maybe save a thousand dollars on a small boat that way.

Fixing Up An Old Lifeboat

Let me tell you a story. In 1974, I got this idea of buying a surplus lifeboat hull and making it into a replica of a Viking trading ship—a "knarr." I got on the surplus bidding list and eventually some boats turned up for sale ranging in size from 18 to 36 feet.

Money was scarce so I bid on the hulls I thought would be least in demand, the big ones. To my amazement, a bid of $125.00 landed me a ten thousand pound steel hull. If ever there was a poor man's route to sailing ecstasy, this was it. A hauling outfit from Rye, New York hauled it home to Rhode Island for $600.00 and there it was—a mammoth grey beached whale of a boat and it was mine all mine. It was my first boat and I was mighty proud of it. I called it the *Odyssey*. The yacht club of Bristol, Rhode Island, watched with a mounting mixture of amusement and glee as I set to work.

The *Odyssey* was 36 feet long and 13 feet across. When I stood in its bottom, I couldn't see out. It was a very big boat and I soon learned that time and labor and money could disappear into such a boat without a trace. Tearing out the rotted seats and the elaborate man-powered propulsion mechanism took the better of a year of Saturdays. The inside was badly rusted. Repairing it took another year and God knows how many dozen bottles of Naval jelly. On any given workday, I could expose an area of bright metal the size of a road map.

It's an impossible task in Bristol, Rhode Island, to rustle up a crew of 20 oarsmen, so I had to come up with an engine. I had a flywheel, a transmission and a propeller already on the boat. To power it, I devised a transverse system of three Briggs and Stratton 5 h.p. motors, each connected by chain to the gearbox through a centrifugal clutch. Crude but bullet proof. When the yacht club next door learned of my intentions, I could hear the laughter all the way over the back fence.

The *Odyssey*, painted dark brown outside and a burnt orange inside, was launched in July of 1976. The power company had donated an enormous aluminum phone pole for a mast. The square sail was tanbark.

The Boats

Man and his "knarr" (PHOTO BY ROBERT ANTON)

View from the deck of the *Odyssey*. The 400-square-foot sail and its yard were supported by two 9-foot posts. Canvas boom tents were to have stretched across the open deck both before and abaft the mast but I was out of funds by then.

The *Odyssey* at her Bristol Harbor mooring.

My father had donated God knows how much paint. The whole enterprise, including three years' storage, had cost more than $3,000, more than I could afford, less than I should have spent.

The first night afloat, a storm came up, pulled up the *Odyssey*'s mooring, and sent her drifting like a vengeful juggernaut through the fleet of yachts in Bristol Harbor. The yacht club, in self defense, tied the *Odyssey* firmly to its dock for the night. Half the club turned out the next day to see the boat motor away. Each Briggs started on the first pull. The big prop churned up a boiling mass of water and the *Odyssey* thrashed its way into Narragansett Bay. As time went by, the chain drive started vibrating badly. Of three chains, one would take the full load; the rest would run slack and raise hob with the sprockets. One chain broke. I repaired it while we ran on the other two engines. Then another chain broke. We raised sail.

For half an hour we experienced the romantic joys of square-rigged sailing. Then we had to get home. We fired up the gang of Briggs and Strattons; the vibration increased. Finally all the chains let go. We drifted by a Rhode Island state mooring and picked it up. The *Odyssey* never left that mooring as long as I owned it. The drive system needed not chains but rubber vee belts and, therefore, a whole new set of clutches and sheaves and fittings. The kitty was dry and my wife was up in arms about all the money I'd spent. Underfinanced all the way, I'd been in over my head from the beginning. Facing that was hard.

The *Odyssey* wintered in the harbor on its mooring, locked in ice. Being an open boat, rain collected in its bilges and turned to ice. Slowly the hull settled further and further under the load. In January, I disconnected the motors and brought them home so they wouldn't drown. When spring came, I put the boat up for sale. During the summer, I rowed a progression of folk out to the *Odyssey*. Each took in the huge investment of work and money remaining to be done and asked quietly to be taken back to shore. In the end, the *Odyssey* was given away—to the Sea Cadets. It took six months to find an organization that would even take it as a gift. It was somewhere in the midst of this experience that I developed my enthusiasm for small boats.

A Happy Story

Several years after the *Odyssey* fiasco, I had another chance at a lifeboat—this time a 12-footer. I found it in a junkyard outside of Boston and purchased it for $100. It once belonged to the tugboat *Jupiter*. The hull just fit into my cellar. Over the winter, I sanded the hull down to bare metal and put on fresh paint, replaced the gunwale, refurbished the wooden seats and made a new rudder. Still interested in square-rigged sailing, I carved a dragon head and tail for the little boat and obtained, through the generosity of a sailmaking class, a red and white striped Viking-style sail. Leeboards were concealed by brightly colored shields that hung from either gunwale. To complement the boat's oar-power, I added a side bracket for a small outboard motor. Authenticity has its limits.

The finished product was christened The *Prince Val* and launched with due ceremony in the spring of 1978. Once it got up headway, it rowed well, and it sailed! Without recutting the sail, I tried it square rigged, lug rigged, and finally, moving the mast forward, sprit rigged.

Fresh from the junkyard—the *Prince Val.*

The *Prince Val* emerges from its winter metamorphosis. Note the steering swivel on the stern quarter for the steering oar.

The *Prince Val* couldn't point too high, but it was fantastic on a reach and downwind. Suddenly Buzzard's Bay was my oyster. The *Prince Val* was simple and rugged. The dragon head drew smiles wherever we went and larger yachts often swung by to toss me a beer and have a gam. Best of all, the *Val* only cost me $200 or so and thus I could experiment and learn without worrying about her much.

I made no real effort to make an overnighter out of the *Prince Val,* though I slept on her deck a night or two under a spare canvas sail. On my longest cruise, I sailed her on a 100-mile ocean trip to Newport, Rhode Island and back. The return sail, with the main boomed out to port and the spare sail set out wing and wing, was one of the highlights of my life. The sky was a crystal blue; the southwest wind whistled up white caps, and we surfed down an endless progression of following seas all the way home.

Eventually I bought a used West Wight Potter and passed the *Prince Val* on (for $100) to a young chap who was eager to take *his* first inexpensive step into sailing.

SAILING ON A MICRO-BUDGET

Student power drives the *Prince Val*. The Viking-style steering oar works!

Prince Val under sail.

Two double-ended dory-like boats tied up near lake St. Jean in northern Quebec. Sometimes boats like this just catch your eye as you drive along . . . and sometimes you can buy one for less than you had dared hope.

The fatal temptation: "I'll give it to you for fifty bucks."

There are derelict small boats in yards all over the country, awaiting your imagination and your love. Don't lose your perspective if you decide to rescue one of these. Keep it cheap and simple. Plan to daysail at first, then, gradually, see if you can figure out a way to camp aboard. Keep your investment of time and money low unless the actual restoration project is going to be a major satisfaction in itself. Keep it fun.

If you build a boat yourself—or refurbish one—don't expect to make a killing when you resell it. Unless you're a master cabinet maker, you'll probably get a very modest return. Price the boat to move out; get your money, and move on.

Check out insurance *before* you buy a kit or get started building your own boat. Make sure you can get insurance. Will the company demand that a marine surveyor examine the boat first? (At *your* expense?) With the *Odyssey,* after searching several weeks, I found a carrier that insured super tankers who agreed to insure the boat as a joke. I never bothered with the *Prince Val.* Check before you buy.

If you plan to trailer your boat, check the hull design. The Luger boats can be purchased with factory-designed trailers. A junkyard salvage job may be harder to match. The *Prince Val,* 12 feet long, weighed *800 pounds!* It would have crushed any trailer built for its size and wallowed around in any trailer built for its weight. A flat-bottomed boat might not fit a standard trailer at all.

Finally, though, take heart. If you've only got a few hundred bucks, you *can* get yourself out on the water. It'll take imagination and a sense of humor but you can do it. If you can avoid giving yourself delusions of grandeur, you can even have fun.

OPEN CRUISING BOATS

J Boats Inc., maker of the famous J24 racers and the new J22, did a market survey and learned that its average owner sails 55 days a year and, of that 55 days, spends only five nights aboard. Not much, even for a racer. It makes you wonder why the builder bothered to put in a cabin and bunks instead of, say, just a tiny private space to go to the bathroom. I suspect the company simply made a marketing decision. The public has a preconceived idea of what a boat is supposed to look like. The public expects a cabin.

What if we abandon the idea of a cabin for a while and think cleverly about this. When you're actually underway, most small boat cabins are an instant passport to nausea and claustrophobia. While you're sailing, in nice weather at least, the cockpit's the thing—the bigger the better. Enter the open boat. The open boat can be *all* cockpit if you want, with room for everybody to sprawl or lounge around and, on a deep boat, even walk around and lean your elbows on the gunwale. If that sounds like fun, it is.

Now night falls. Bugs come out. It looks like rain—now what? Maybe you park the boat for the night and go ashore, either to your home, to a motel or to a tent pitched on shore. That works some places but not everywhere. Many shorelines are privately owned. You can't just sail into Marion Harbor and start roasting weenies on the Saltonstall's front lawn. Hospitality has its limits. Why not pitch your tent over the boat itself? Now that big walkaround space becomes a cabin in which to cook, play cards, and sleep. You've got the best of both worlds.

In the past several years, a number of manufacturers, mostly in Florida and along the Gulf Coast, have begun marketing some appealing open cruisers. Some have partial cabins open to the cockpit; some have decked-over sections with hatches that, when opened, reveal galleys and toilets and other practical cruising necessities. Some have dodgers that pull up like the cover on a baby carriage at night and then fold down out of the way by day. It's a wide-open field with many attractive and ingenious designs for those willing to accept alternatives to the preconception of what a cruising boat is "supposed" to look like. Let's look at a couple of designs that have gained a following and promise to be around awhile.

The Dovekie

Edey & Duff, Inc.
15 Harbor Road
Mattapoisett, MA 02739

The Dovekie by Edey & Duff boatbuilders, Mattapoisett, Massachusetts is a 21-foot vessel, the product of Phil Bolger's inventive mind and Peter Duff's molding talent and marketing courage. The Dovekie is highly unconventional and yet, in its own way, very traditional. The sail rig, a triangular sprit, goes back more than 100 years. The Dutch used leeboards 400 years ago. They're simple, efficient, and they open up the cabin interior where a centerboard trunk would be a major nuisance. The Dovekie draws only four inches with leeboards raised and so it will go anywhere. With such shallow draft, it's easy to row and so oarports have been provided—an idea about 4,000 years old. The cockpit melts into a partially enclosed "cabin" that has several generous molded in skylights. Canvas panels close up the "cabin" and cockpit at night into a spacious sheltered area. The whole boat weighs only 600 pounds. There's no arguing the Dovekie is unconventional but if you are too, and the features appeal, you may have met your match.

The enormous interior of the Dovekie 21.

Dovekie under sail

Here's a clever idea. The Dovekie mounts its outboard motor on the rudder. When the rudder turns, so does the motor.

Marsh Hen underway. Note "brailing" lines running to the mast—for reefing. (inset) Mud Hen with dodger up

Florida Bay Boat Co.
270 N.W. 73 Street
Miami, FL 35150

   The Mud Hen is built by Ruben Trane and the Florida Bay Boat Co.,
Miami, Florida. Trane started off by designing a fairly traditional flat-
bottom sharpie-style hull. From this point he has gone modular, giving
the prospective owner the pleasurable opportunity of designing the rest
of the boat. If an owner wants an *African Queen*-style motorboat with
the entire boat covered by a canvas roof trimmed with tassles, he can
order it that way. If he or she wants it's possible to order a canvas dodger
to turn the forward half of the boat into a rainproof, bugproof shelter.
Other options are a fiberglass trunk cabin with portholes, or in the
"Marsh Hen" configuration, molded-in storage areas. Both models have
centerboard and, at 17 feet, offer extreme shallow draft. Want more
room? Trane has a 21-foot version—the Bay Hen. All versions offer a
variety of sail plans and sail shapes, too. I like buyer's choice. The only
choices most manufacturers offer are hull and sail color—even then at
extra cost. Choice in areas other than the cosmetic is rare.

The Marsh Hen

The Bay Hen under sail

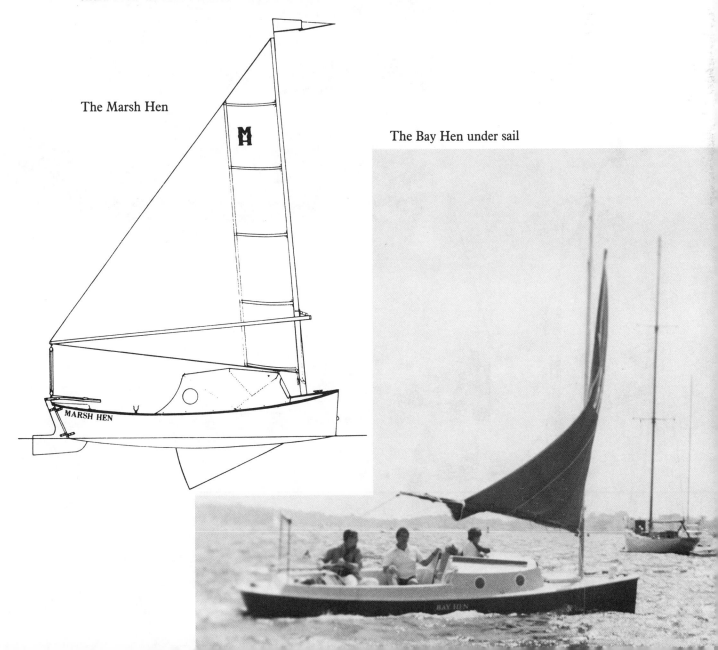

The Sea Pearl

Marine Concepts
159 Oakwood St. E
Tarpon Springs, FL 33589

The Sea Pearl 21, by Marine Concepts in Tarpon Springs, Florida, is a traditional whaleboat or peapod shape rendered into fiberglass. Here's a long sleek hull, easy to row, easy to drive under sail. The hull is less beamy than some of the other boats we've considered so far. It has an optional dodger to create overnight shelter. Like the Dovekie, the Sea Pearl uses leeboards to reduce leeway under sail. Here too, the buyer has options: the boat can be equipped with either wishbone sails or lug sails.

The overnight dodger on the Sea Pearl. Note the lee boards.

The Sea Pearl

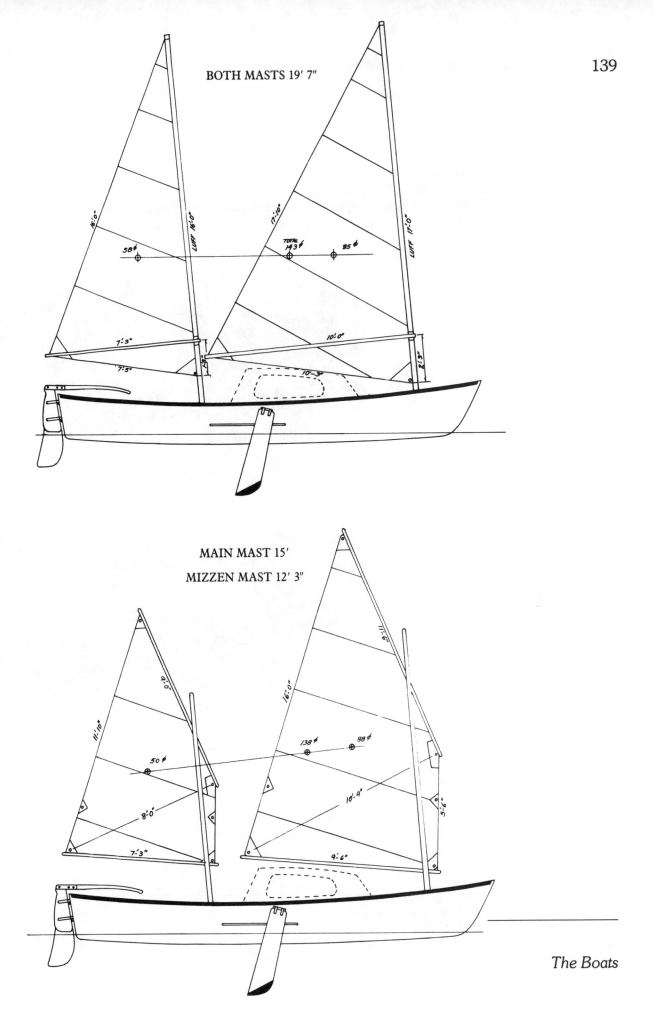

BOTH MASTS 19′ 7″

MAIN MAST 15′

MIZZEN MAST 12′ 3″

The Boats

The Beachcomber Dory

Beachcomber Boats
Box 206
Port Salerno, FL 33492

The Beachcomber Dory, by Beachcomber Boat Building Co., Port Salerno, Florida, is another small open boat of very traditional design. We've looked at a modern version of a Greek galley, a sharpie, a whale boat, and now a lapstrake dory rendered in fiberglass. This 18-footer also is available with a large dodger for shelter and bug protection.

The Beachcomber Dory

The Beachcomber Dory under sail

Summary

These are some though certainly not all of the small open cruising boats being manufactured at the time of this writing. Many of these manufacturers are small outfits. I hope they'll grow and prosper. New companies will surely continue to come into being and those least competitive will continue to vanish away. Still, the open cruising boat is a very compelling concept with a lot of potential for growth. If you're looking for a boat, don't overlook this category; and if you're looking to convert an existing open boat for cruising, they offer you a wealth of ideas to borrow from.

Does this approach—the open cruiser—have any drawbacks? Certainly. Are they serious? It depends on what kind of sailing you are planning to do. Many of these designs are flat-bottomed—ideal for exploring coves and backwaters and hidden beaches. In rough open water, flat bottoms will pound and have a hard time of it, generally. Open boats, if swamped, are not self-bailing and often are not self-righting. They may not sink, but they'll be harder to bail out. An open-water sailor may prefer a smaller self-bailing cockpit, even though he pays for it in space and comfort. Still Drascombe, an English firm, makes a family of seagoing open boats that boast an impressive history of ocean voyages. Some of these are keel designs, others feature shallow keels and bilge keels. These boats are tough and very capable.

At this writing, Webb Chiles is completing his around the world cruise on his Drascombe Lugger, a testimony to the rugged quality of both the boat and the man. Chiles has written several books and numerous articles on his adventures.

The deep open interior of the Old World 18 offers the ultimate in daysailing. A boom tent turns this into an easy overnighter. Look at the floor space!

Some canvas dodgers protect a cabin when the boat is riding at anchor —facing the wind—but admit water when it's tied at dockside or on a trailer, when the wind and rain may come from astern.

No one approach is intrinsically superior; it all depends on what kind of sailing you want to do and where you want to do it. If most of your sailing will be daysailing, or if you plan to camp out ashore a lot, the open cruiser could very well be your best choice.

The Old World 18 has traditional lines and a boom and gaff rig.

The Boats

If there's an area in the marketplace that needs development, this is it. In terms of razzle-dazzle sailing, multi-hull sailing is the new frontier, with speed and excitement galore. Alas, in the price ranges we're discussing in this book, there's not much around. Let me suggest a simple approach to get started. If you own a small catamaran already, say a Hobie 16, this might be something you could try. Maybe you could build something like this as an accessory:

Adapting a Small Catamaran for Cruising

Out of plywood or even fiberglass, fashion a long, lightweight unit to fit across the twin hulls—just ahead of the trampoline frame. In the very center of this "cruising module," where its weight is evenly distributed, put a lightweight portable head. To the left put a countertop, small propane stove, and storage for a small supply of food. To the right, add storage for a nylon tent, sleeping bags, and perhaps a change of clothes. A series of lids provide protection from spray as well as a smooth aerodynamic appearance. That's all you need. By day, with a minor weight penalty, you have an unencumbered high speed boat with twice the cruising range of anything remotely its size. At night, the cat can easily be beached or anchored in shallow water. A boom tent snaps in place

Speed's the thing! Boston Whaler's Supercat.

over the leading edge of the "cruising module" and covers the entire trampoline area. Now you have a private and sheltered area to cook and sleep. Simple and Spartan of course, but no more so than a micro cruiser and certainly with vastly superior sailing performance and sleeping space. An 18-foot catamaran can cost no more than many micro cruisers and can sail literally three times as fast. It's an intriguing thought.

Small Cruising Multi-hulls

The only other relatively inexpensive multi-hull cruiser is the Tremolino—a trimaran. The Tremolino offers a central hull with micro cruiser style accommodations, which can be straddled by either two Hobie 16 hulls (if you wanted to convert your Hobie 16) or by two hulls of Tremolino's manufacture. The rig was designed by veteran multi-hull architect Dick Newick and, as one might expect, has won its share of races. In cost, the complete boat compares with that of most compact cruisers.

In the price range of most family weekenders are two more possibilities, the Reynolds 21 catamaran and the Australian-built Tramp, a trimaran.

The Reynolds 21 is a catamaran of sufficient size to offer a small cabin in each hull. Two bunks occupy most of the interior space in each hull. You get four slender bunks in all and modest storage space. What you *do* get, of course, is blistering speed—up to 20 knots!

The Tremolino trimaran

The Reynolds 21

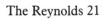

The Boats

The Tramp is an 18-foot multi-hull daysailer with a fair turn of speed and, with almost 15 feet of beam, unbelievable stability. It can daysail up to six and, with an optional boom tent, sleep up to four. For transportation, its outer hulls hinge downward to a folded total beam of eight feet—a trailerable width. The enormous trampolines offer 100 square feet of lounging space.

From here on in, cruising multi-hulls go drastically upward in price. Like the open cruising boats, these boats, despite their high speed allure, represent a tiny fraction of the boat market as a whole. Their general design concepts may prove more durable than their manufacturers, though I hope not. Real innovators deserve to get rich. I guess we'll see.

The Tramp trimaran (inset) An enormous cockpit tent turns the Tramp into a spacious overnighter.

Stiletto's optional bridgedeck tent encloses entire bridgedeck and provides additional living space for a boatload of guests.

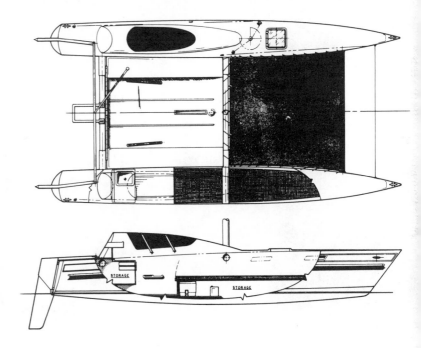

Why, might you ask, do multi-hull cruisers constitute such a small segment of the market? There may be several reasons:

Small catamarans are ideal daysailers. Most Americans will not forego their comforts and so, though they'll spend a fair penny for a high speed daysailer, they'll spend a lot more money for a boat they can cruise in with style and comfort. People think of catamarans as seagoing fighter-planes, not as something to spend the night in.

Sailing in catamarans can be a wet and hairy experience. Little children might be scared rigid and hate it. Lacking a deep protective cockpit, most catamarans are not considered "family" boats. They require athletic skill and a willingness to fly high—to take chances. That's not for everybody. Still, there's room for growth, especially if a class of cruising people develops who are willing to rough it a little to get out on the water.

The Boats

A more expensive multihull rocketship, the Stiletto 27 offers great speed and superior accommodations.

At the time of this writing, the trend in America is towards bigger boats. Perhaps the rich are getting richer and the poor are getting poorer. I hope that's not true. I suspect it has more to do with our attitudes about affluence and luxury. I'd like to talk you into bucking the trend. I'd like to talk you into thinking small and simple, knowing that if you select compactness and simplicity, you'll sail more and worry less. As a demonstration of what can be accomplished in a small space, I want to direct your attention to a world cruiser only 20 feet long—the Flicka.

In price, the Flicka is way out of the parameters of this book; it's as soundly built as any private yacht you could find on any ocean anywhere. You pay for that. But just look at her! Standing headroom in just 20 feet. A full galley where you can whip up meals of some sophistication, a head and shower compartment, and generous bunks. A couple could actually *live* on this thing if they wanted to and sail around the world. When you think small, everything else is reduced to manageable proportions: the sails are small, cheap to repair or replace. You don't need much bottom paint. A small and inexpensive outboard is all the power you need—and maybe you can get away without even that. Insurance fees are small; dockage fees are low. You can haul the boat behind your car. You don't need winches and other fancy knick-knacks. In each and every way, your cares are reduced while your satisfactions stay nearly the same.

WHICH BOAT FOR YOU?

How could I summarize for you all that we've said about these many different kinds of boats? Let's begin by saying that the choice you make will largely be determined by the kind of sailing you plan to do, the number of people you plan to take with you, the waters you plan to sail in, and the distance you will have to travel to get to the water. Let's review the choices from these perspectives.

BOAT TYPE	KIND OF SAILING/ SIZE OF CREW	SAILING CONDITIONS	DISTANCE TO TRAVEL	COST
Micro Cruiser	daysails 4 cruises 2 voyages 1	Lakes, bays, rivers, most common fair-moderate winds. A few are capable of ocean sailing.	The best choice if you must haul over long distances.	least expensive
Compact Cruiser	daysails 4 cruises 2–4 voyages 1–2	Lakes, bays, rivers, most common fair-moderate winds. A few are capable of ocean sailing.	Still light enough to haul and launch fairly easily.	more expensive
Open Cruiser	daysails up to 6 cruises 2–4 extended cruises 1–2	Most are designed for inland and coastal sailing in fair-moderate winds.	Still light enough to haul and launch easily.	more expensive
Family Weekender	daysails up to 6 cruises 4 extended cruises 2	Most are designed for comfortable inland and coastal sailing in fair-moderate winds.	Portable but more demanding to trailer and launch.	most expensive
Cruising Multi-hull	daysails 4–6 cruises 1–2 extended cruises 1–2	Mostly designed for high-speed inland and coastal sailing in fair-moderate winds.	Portable but more demanding to trailer and launch.	most expensive

Very high priced but, at 20 feet, maybe the ultimate small boat: Pacific Seacraft's Flicka.

SAILING ON A
MICRO-BUDGET

Liveaboard potential in 20 feet: the Flicka.

If I were to identify a single most endearing characteristic of each type, I'd like the micro cruiser for its wonderful ease of transportation and operation. Everything is so easy. The compact cruiser is my favorite all-around compromise choice. You can squeeze in a family of four; you can still haul it around fairly easily, and the price is still within the reach of most families. The open cruiser is the most comfortable daysailer of the group because of its open spaciousness. Many are still easily covered over at night. Also I like the wide choice in designs available. The family weekender is wonderful if you can afford it and don't have to haul it too far. I've seen some I could even consider living on for a stretch of time. It's not a boat I would recommend for repeated hauling into and out of the water. The cruising multi-hull's greatest appeal is its speed. Comfort overnight and portability are only moderately good; it's the sailing that would turn the multi-hull enthusiast on more than anything else.

One last thing. Some boats just appeal to you because . . . well, they just do. For some reason, they conform to your idea of what a small boat should look like. Personally, I'm attracted by the convertible charms of open cruising boats yet, maybe irrationally, I like a cabin with grab rails on the roof. A cabin means security to me. This is wholly irrational, but there it is. I owned a family weekender once but got tired of hauling it around and, under sail, found it too big. Nice boat, though . . . lots of room. Evidently, my concept of an ideal boat involves something quite little. Your ideals will be different of course, wholly unique to you. So browse around a lot; look at lots of pictures; go to as many boat shows as you can, and listen to your irrational heart. Despite all the practical considerations, the boat you see when you close your eyes is the one you really want.

CONCLUSION

It's a snowy Sunday afternoon. Bored with football, I turn off the set and wander to the window. The storm continues unabated; snow sifts through the trees, rumbles from the roofs, blankets the ground.

Bundled in my coat and boots, I clomp through the kitchen on my way outdoors. A pot steams; my wife looks up. "Going to visit the boat?" I'm continually stunned by how well she knows me.

Outdoors I don't notice the cold so much as the silence. I plow twin furrows to the garage and feel the satisfying crunch under my feet. I pound back a wedge of snow with the garage door and slip inside. All around the edges of the open door, snowflakes flutter and catch the silver light. Inside the garage, sound is muffled. There is *Fearless*, blocked up on the earth floor. Her white decks are dusty and pigeons have spattered her here and there. I slide a gloved hand along her bow. Oddly, when I try to remember summertime voyages, no images come. I peer into the smoked plastic windows but see nothing. A gust of wind buffets the building; snow swirls in through the shaft of light. I let myself out. It's bright. I fasten the latch and tramp squinting back to the kitchen door.

"How was it?" my wife asks. My boots are already making puddles on the floor. I step in one, feel the wet cold soaking through my stocking and pull my foot back in annoyance. My glasses fog up. "It's OK." Without knowing why, I'm confused. Not knowing why I went out, it's hard to say how it was. Why exactly *did* I go out?

I guess I really wanted to "visit" with my boat, as my wife put it. When we trust our lives to a product of our own hands, maybe we still have that ancient need to believe that the thing has a soul—so we can trust it, talk to it when we get scared, thank it for safe passages. In the age of fiberglass, maybe we need that old superstition more than ever.

It's getting dark out. The streetlight illuminates a cone of falling snow. I lie down and take a nap. As I close my eyes, I imagine it's summer and I'm aboard. In my mind's eye I visualize the cabin. I know where everything is. I know exactly where I can reach out and touch Bettina's shoulder. If I slide open the hatch, I'll have a patch of stars that swing in lazy arcs in and out of view until I'm tranced into sleep. What more could anyone want?

The Boats

CENTERBOARD	KEEL/CENTER-BOARD	SHOAL KEEL	FULL KEEL	OTHER
		MICRO CRUISERS		
West Wight Potter 15 Gloucester 16 Neptune 16	Montgomery 15	Compac 16 Victoria 18	North Shore 9 Nordica 16	
		COMPACT CRUISERS		

Rinkerbuilt 16
Luger 16 (kit)
Holder 17
Siren 17
Skipper's Mate 17
Cape Cod Catboat 17
Nauset Catboat 18
Marshall Sanderling 18
Montego 19
Gloucester 19
Gloucester 20
Hunter 20
Mirage 20
Triton 21
MacGregor 21
Bay Hen 21
	Balboa 16
	Slipper 17
	  (option)
	Montgomery 17
	Ranger 18
	O'Day 19
	Starwind 19
		Slipper 17
		Sovereign 17
		Renken 18
		Skipper 20
		Montego 20
		Compac 19
			Cape Dory Typhoon
			Cape Cod Golden
			  Eye
			Boston Whaler 20
			  (Harpoon)
				West Wight Potter 19
				  (drop keel)
				Holder 20
				  (drop keel)

		FAMILY WEEKENDERS		

San Juan 21
Sirius 21
Hunter 22
Catalina 22
MacGregor 22
MacGregor 25
	Luger 21 (kit)
	Starwind 22
	O'Day 22
	Gloucester 22
	Tanzer 22
		Alcar 22	Freedom 21
			J-22
			Tanzer 22
			  (fin keel version)
			Hunter 22
				Merit 22
				  (drop keel)
				Holder 20
				  (drop keel)

		OPEN CRUISERS		

Dockrell 17
Marsh Hen 17
Mud Hen 17
Old World 18
Beach Comber Dory 18
Lightfoot 21
	Ranger 20			Drascombe Skaffie
				Drascombe Lugger
				  (bilge keels)
				Sea Pearl 21
				Dovekie 21
				  (lee boards)

		MULTI-HULL CRUISERS		
Tramp 20 Trimaran Reynolds 21 Catamaran Tremolino 22 Trimaran				